THE NAKED NOW

There are two trees in the middle of the garden, the tree of life and the tree of the knowledge of good and evil.

— Genesis 2:9 —

THE NAKED NOW

Learning to See
as the Mystics See

RICHARD ROHR

A Crossroad Book
The Crossroad Publishing Company
New York

This printing: 2013

The Crossroad Publishing Company
www.CrossroadPublishing.com

In continuation of our 200-year tradition of independent publishing, The Crossroad Publishing Company proudly offers a variety of books with strong, original voices and diverse perspectives. The viewpoints expressed in our books are not necessarily those of The Crossroad Publishing Company, any of its imprints or of its employees. No claims are made or responsibility assumed for any health or other benefit.

Printed in the United States of America.

The text of this book is set in 12/15.5 Bulmer.

Library of Congress Cataloging-in-Publication Data

Rohr, Richard.
    The naked now : learning to see as the mystics see / Richard Rohr.
      p. cm.
    Includes bibliographical references.
    ISBN-13: 978-0-8245-2543-9 (alk. paper)
    ISBN-10: 0-8245-2543-4 (alk. paper)
    1. Mysticism. 2. Spiritual life – Christianity. I. Title.
BV5082.3.R64 2009
248.2′2 – dc22   2009030838

Contents

PART TWO

PART THREE

Appendices
PRACTICING THE NAKED NOW

Why I Am Writing This Book

*No man can say his eyes have had enough of seeing, his ears
their fill of hearing.* — ECCLESIASTES 1:8

I am a man born between ages, moving between cultures, seeing
between religions, but also happily a Christian. I love what I see:
life excites me. Yet I know there is still so much more to see and
hear, so much more to know and do. This seeing is also painful,
and there are things I wish I did not see, or did not know.

I was born in the middle of Middle America, Kansas, in the
middle of the Great War (1943), into a German Catholic family
with deeply conservative farm roots, and yet I was sent to be educated into a much larger, rapidly changing and reforming world
of the 1960s. Vatican Council II tried to reform Catholicism; the
therapeutic movement tried to reform the psyche; and the War
Against Poverty and the civil rights and antiwar movements tried
to reform America.

I have been told that I have a fixation for trying to see almost
all things as both/and — or as a "collision of opposites." It feels
as though it is written in my genes — my worst mistakes come
from not self-balancing. If you believe in astrological signs, I was
born on the cusp of Pisces, where the two fish move in opposite
directions, on the day between winter and spring, in the year in
which the Resurrection was celebrated on its latest possible date.
I am always waiting for Easter, but surely expecting it too. I was

ordained in a Catholic Church on the very site of Stone's Folly in Topeka, Kansas, seventy years after they began speaking in tongues at that spot in 1900. I was always happily Catholic but curiously Protestant and Pentecostal. I knew early on that there were different kinds of knowing. Words divided reality between either and or, but my living experience was always both-and.

I can survive only by trying to build bridges, both affirming and also denying most of my own ideas and those of others. Most people tend to see me as highly progressive, yet I would say I am, in fact, a values conservative and a process liberal. I believe in justice, truth, follow-through, honesty, personal and financial responsibility, faithful love, and humility — all deeply traditional values. Yet, in my view, you need to be imaginative, radical, dialogical, and even countercultural to live these values at any depth. Whether in church life or politics, neither conservatives nor liberals are doing this very well today. Both are too dualistic — they do not think or see like the mystics.

I am formed by twentieth-century American culture, for good and for ill, by Catholic theology, for good and for ill, and by the wisdom traditions of the Native and world religions — especially Franciscanism, which has been largely for the good. It is that "perennial philosophy," as Aldous Huxley called it, that I hope to draw upon in this book, along with insights from developmental psychology, theology, philosophy, history, the mystics of all religions, community-building experiences, and the giving and receiving of spiritual direction.

Primarily I am concerned here with why people do not see very well — and how we perhaps can. What is it that keeps us humans from reading reality truthfully, humbly, and helpfully? Why do we — including people at the highest levels of church, education, and state — appear to be so imprisoned in ourselves? In effect, why have the world religions stopped doing their job of spiritually transforming people and cultures? Why have we told people they must "believe" in God in order to experience God, when God is clearly at work in ways that many "eyes have not seen, nor ears have heard, nor has it entered into our minds" (1 Corinthians 2:9)?

Along with the resources already mentioned, I will draw upon my own journey of trying to see myself and my world honestly, more lovingly, and in ever broader and less self-serving frames. Much of what I see comes from my own mistakes too numerous to count. Failure, sin, humiliation, and shadow work are very good teachers if we allow them to be. I present this investigation in a series of ways, including reflections, stories, sayings, interpretations from Hebrew and Christian Scriptures, and finally concrete practices. This book can be read from cover to cover, but you may also prefer to read one section at a time and reflect on how the message relates to your own seeing. Pick a chapter heading that seems to speak to you, because many of them can stand alone.

All of the issues above have led me to the overall message in this book:

ALL SAYING MUST BE BALANCED BY UNSAYING, and knowing must be humbled by unknowing. Without this balance, religion invariably becomes arrogant, exclusionary, and even violent.

ALL LIGHT MUST BE INFORMED BY DARKNESS, and all success by suffering. St. John of the Cross called this Luminous Darkness, St. Augustine, the Paschal Mystery or the necessary Passover, and Catholics proclaim it loudly as *the* mystery of faith at every Eucharist. Yet it is seldom an axiom at the heart of our lives.

The early but learned pattern of dualistic thinking can get us only so far; so all religions at the more mature levels have discovered another "software" for processing the really big questions, like death, love, infinity, suffering, and God. Many of us call this access "contemplation." *It is a nondualistic way of seeing the moment.* Originally, the word was simply "prayer."

It is living in the naked now, the "sacrament of the present moment," that will teach us how to actually experience our experiences, whether good, bad, or ugly, and how to let them transform us. Words by themselves will invariably divide the moment; pure presence lets it be what it is, as it is.

When you can be present, you will know the Real Presence. I promise you this is true.

And it is almost that simple.

March 20, 2008
Holy Thursday

THE NAKED NOW

PART ONE

CHAPTER ONE

The Gift Is Already Given

Our hope is not deceptive. The love of God has been poured into our hearts by the Holy Spirit that has been given to us.
— ROMANS 5:5

You already know. The Spirit is with you and the Spirit is in you.
— JOHN 14:17

The future is by definition the unsayable and the uncontrollable, filled with paradoxes, mysteries, and confusions. It is an imperfect world at every level. Therefore the future is always, somehow, scary. We attempt to build for ourselves many protections against this imperfection, even in the patterns of our mind. This unsayable future — preparing for it and also fearing it — determines much of our lives. Thus we search for predictability, explanation, and order to give ourselves some sense of peace and control.

Even much of religion itself has become a search for social order, group cohesion, and personal worthiness, or a way of escaping into the next world, which unfortunately destroys most of its transformative power. True spirituality is not a search for perfection or control or the door to the next world; it is a search for divine union *now.* The great discovery is always that what we are searching for has already been given! I did not find it; it found me. It is Jacob's shout of *Eureka!* at the foot of his ladder to heaven in Genesis 28:16–17.

Union and perfection are two different journeys with very different strategies. Common religion seeks private perfection; the mystics seek and enjoy the foundation itself — divine union, totally given. Personal perfection insists on private knowing and certitude. Surprisingly, union is a much better way of knowing. It is *a shared knowing* that is much more solid and consoling. I promise you that this will make more sense as the book unfolds, but in the meantime just ask anyone in love if this is not true.

The most amazing fact about Jesus, unlike almost any other religious founder, is that he found God in *disorder and imperfection* — and told us that we must do the same or we would never be content on this earth. This is what makes Jesus so counterintuitive to most eras and cultures, and why most never perceived the great good news in this utter shift of consciousness. That failure to understand his core message, and a concrete program by which you could experience this truth for yourself, is at the center of our religious problem today. We looked for hope where it was never promised, and no one gave us the proper software so we could know hope for ourselves, least of all in disorder and imperfection! Worst of all, we did not know that *hope and union are the same thing,* and that real hope has nothing to do with mental certitudes.

WHEN YOU SURRENDER
TO FEAR AND DISTRACTION

If you surrender to the fear of uncertainty, life can become a set of insurance policies. Your short time on this earth becomes small and self-protective, a kind of circling of the wagons around what you can be sure of and what you think you can control — even God. It provides you with the illusion that you are in the driver's seat, navigating on safe, small roads, and usually in a single, predetermined direction that can take you only where you have already been.

For far too many people, no life journey is necessary because we think we already have all our answers at the beginning. "The church says, . . . the Bible says, etc."

A second group tries a different approach. They choose to whistle in the dark, look the other way, or just keep busy — seeking various ways of being important, or as Jesus put it, trying to "build bigger barns." For them, life becomes a series of manufactured dramas, entertainment, and diversionary tactics intended to help them avoid the substantial questions. Here, what some call *intensity* is frequently an avoidance of what I will call *presence* — intimacy with ourselves, with life, and with others. This avoidance is symbolized by what we call the consumer culture, which in our current economic situation appears to be falling apart.

This group also represents a large percentage of humanity, especially in the developed world. Governments encourage this pacification by various distractions, what used to be called "bread and circuses." They know it will keep us small, content, and uninterested in those "weightier matters of the law: justice, mercy, and good faith" (Matthew 23:23) that have attracted all great souls.

A third group does seek various forms of transcendence and spirituality, but in a mixture of mature and immature ways. One major theme in this book is that, unfortunately, so much religious seeking today is immature transcendence, dualistically split off from any objective experience of union with God, self, or others — what Owen Barfield would have called "the desert of nonparticipation."[1]

If it is authentically experienced, Christianity is *the overcoming of the split from God's side once and for all!* Sadly, most of us remain split inside of a heady set of formulas and religious jargon, a place where deep constant hope cannot be found — to say nothing of joy. We need to leave the desert for a much better land, a "final participation" that can be partially enjoyed now.

WHEN YOU JOYFULLY SURRENDER TO GOD

Mature transcendence is an actual "falling into" and an "undergoing" of God, as James Alison so brilliantly names it.[2] God is "done unto us," and all we can do is allow it, as both the similar prayers of Mary at the Annunciation and Jesus in the Garden of Gethsemane make clear. What we fall into is what Christianity would call both "an abyss" and an "utter foundation." What a paradox! But in God, they are not opposites.

When we do get there, we almost wonder how we got there. We know we did not *do* anything nearly as much as we know we were *done unto.* We are being utterly and warmly held and falling helplessly into a scary mystery at the very same time — caught between profound desire and the question, "Where is this going to take me?" It has been said many times that, after transformation, you seldom have the feeling you have found anything. It feels much more like Someone found you!

You find yourself having been grabbed, being held, and being Someone's beloved. At first, you do not even know what is going on. All you know is that it is a most wondrous undergoing, but an undergoing nevertheless. You know you have been "had" (see Jeremiah 20:7–9 or Isaiah 6:4–7). You are in Someone Else's grip. How else will anybody freely and rightly give up control? They won't. They'll use religion itself as a disguised way of taking control, or try to control God by their good behavior.

Finally you allow yourself to stand before *one* mirror for your identity — you surrender to the naked now of true prayer and full presence. You become a Thou before the great I AM. Such ultimate mirroring gives you the courage to leave other mirrors behind you. "Human approval means nothing to me," Jesus said. "Why do you waste time looking to one another for approval when you have the approval that comes from the One God?" (John 5:41, 44). Henceforward, as Teresa of Avila said, "You find God in yourself and yourself in God," a discovery that precedes, outdoes, and undercuts all of the best psychology in the world. Think of the thousands of dollars you can save in therapy!

Most people in our whimsical culture live in a hall of mirrors, and so we find ourselves with fragile and rapidly changing identities, needing a lot of affirmation. We see this especially in so many young people. Their identities are built on feelings, moods, and ideas that are easily manipulated by everything around them, including advertising and its selling of superficial images.[3]

You have been given something so much better, so much more joyful and more substantial than that! Divine presence, and the faith, hope, and love that accompany it, are a gift — you cannot control it — but nevertheless a gift that can and should be asked for (Luke 11:13). *Asking for something from God does not mean talking God into it; it means an awakening of the gift within ourselves.* You only ask for something you have already begun to taste! The gift has already been given. Most people, quite sadly and with disastrous consequences, do not know that the gift is already theirs. The teachers of the early Christian centuries, along with many of the later saints and mystics, were clear about this. Yet most Christians today still seem to be like the citizens of Ephesus in apostolic days, saying in effect, "We did not even know there was such a thing as the Holy Spirit" (Acts 19:2).

DISCOVER YOUR BIRTHRIGHT

It's true that you cannot risk telling people with an immature or dualistic consciousness about the Great Indwelling before they have actually experienced it, because they will always abuse it or trivialize it for purposes of superiority, libertinism, or control. This is probably what Jesus meant by one of his more offensive images, "throwing pearls before swine" (Matthew 7:6). At the same time, we surely did not have to deny it or keep it such a big secret! Perhaps this occurred because many of the clergy had themselves never experienced divine union and so could not teach others about it. Catholics and Orthodox make the Holy Spirit depend on membership and sacraments; Protestants make the Spirit depend on a personal decision or faith as a technique.

In both cases, *we* are back in charge; *we* are the doers. There is no undergoing.

Only people who have undergone some level of conversion can be told they have the Holy Spirit and be prepared to understand what one is talking about. Life will then "fan it into flame" (2 Timothy 1:6), but they will always and forever know that the fire was given from Elsewhere. There is absolutely nothing you can do to earn or get the Holy Spirit; there is nothing at all you can do to attain the divine indwelling (e.g., Romans 8:10, Galatians 3:1–5).[4] Don't try to "believe" in the Holy Spirit as one doctrine among others. Instead, *practice drawing from this deep well within you,* and then you will naturally believe. Put the horse first, and it will draw the cart.

At the same time, there is nothing you can do to *lose* the Holy Spirit; the most you can do, as Ephesians cleverly says, is to "grieve" the existing Presence that is "sealed" within you (4:30). You can, therefore, be ignorant of your birthright. You can neglect the gift, and thus not enjoy its wonderful fruits. That seems to be the case with many people, and is what we mean by "sinners." The word signifies not moral inferiors so much as people who do not know *who* they are and *whose* they are, people who have no connection to their inherent dignity and importance. They have to struggle for it by all kinds of futile performances. What a waste. Thus, do not hate "sinners" or look down on them. Feel sorry for what they are missing out on!

Why do we have this gift and yet not realize it? Perhaps God does not want to force anything on us that we do not actually desire or choose for ourselves. So a lovely dance ensues between God and the soul that preserves freedom on both sides.

The gift is objectively already within, and yet has to be desired and awakened by the person. But you never know that it is within until after it is awakened! This is another paradox. Faith is often *clarified and joy-filled hindsight — after we have experienced our experiences.* But the path ahead still demands walking in trust, risk, and various degrees of darkness. Henceforth, you will remember in the darkness what you once experienced in the light. But the path ahead will always be a necessary mixture of darkness and light.

In the Judeo-Christian creation story, humans were created in the very "image and likeness of God" (Genesis 1:26). Our DNA is divine. The divine indwelling is never earned by any behavior whatsoever or any ritual, but only *recognized* and *realized* (Romans 11:6, Ephesians 2:8–10) and fallen in love with. When you are ready, you will be both underwhelmed and overwhelmed at the boundless mystery of your own humanity. You will know you are standing under the same waterfall of mercy as everybody else and receiving an undeserved *radical* grace, which gets to the *root* of everything. Without that underlying experience of God as both *abyss* and *ground,* it is almost impossible to live in the now, in the fullness of who I am, warts and all, and almost impossible to experience the Presence that, paradoxically, always fills the abyss and shakes the ground.

PRAYER — PRACTICING HEAVEN NOW

"Everything exposed to the light itself becomes light," says Ephesians 5:14. In prayer, we merely keep returning the divine gaze and we become its reflection, almost in spite of ourselves (2 Corinthians 3:18). The word "prayer" has often been trivialized by making it into a way of getting what you want. But in this book, I use "prayer" as the umbrella word for *any interior journeys or practices that allow you to experience faith, hope, and love within yourself.* It is not a technique for getting things, a pious exercise that somehow makes God happy, or a requirement for entry into heaven. It is much more like practicing heaven now.

The essential religious experience is that you are being "known through" more than knowing anything in particular yourself. Yet despite this difference, it will feel like true knowing. Throughout this book, we will interchangeably call this new way of knowing contemplation, nondualistic thinking, or "third-eye" seeing. Such prayer, such seeing, takes away your anxiety about figuring it all out fully for yourself, or needing to be right about your formulations. At this point, God becomes more a verb than a noun, more a process than a conclusion, more an experience than a dogma, more a personal relationship than an idea.[5] There is Someone dancing with you, and you are not afraid of making mistakes.

No wonder all of the great liturgical prayers of the churches end with the same phrase: "through Christ our Lord, Amen." *We do not pray to Christ; we pray through Christ.* Or even more precisely, Christ prays through us. We are always and forever the conduits, the instruments, the tuning forks, the receiver stations (Romans 8:22–27). We slowly learn the right frequencies that pick up the signal. The core task of all good spirituality is to teach us to "cooperate" with what God already wants to do and has already begun to do (Romans 8:28). In fact, nothing good would even enter our minds unless in the previous moment God had not already "moved" within us. We are always and forever merely seconding the motion.

To live in such a way is to live inside of an unexplainable hope, because your life will now feel much larger than your own. In fact, it is not your own life, and yet, paradoxically, you are more "you" than ever before. That is the constant and consistent experience of the mystics — their vision that can also be your own. "God, you were here all along, and I never knew it" (Genesis 28:16).

CHAPTER TWO

The Great Unsaying

Do not utter the name of God in vain.
— EXODUS 20:7

I cannot emphasize enough the momentous importance of the Jewish revelation of the name of God. It puts the entire nature of our spirituality in correct context and, if it had been followed, could have freed us from much idolatry and arrogance. As we now spell and pronounce it, the word is *Yahweh*. For those speaking Hebrew, it was the Sacred Tetragrammaton YHVH (*yod, he, vav,* and *he*). It was considered a literally unspeakable word for Jews, and any attempt to know what we were talking about was "in vain," as the commandment said (Exodus 20:7). Instead, they used *Elohim* or *Adonai* in speaking or writing. From God's side the divine identity was kept mysterious and unavailable to the mind; when Moses asked for the divinity's name, he got only the phrase that translates something to this effect: "I AM WHO AM. . . . This is my name forever; this is my title for all generations" (Exodus 3:14–15).

This unspeakability has long been recognized, but we now know it goes even deeper: formally the word was not spoken at all, but *breathed!* Many are convinced that its correct pronunciation is an attempt to replicate and imitate the very sound of inhalation and exhalation.[6] The one thing we do every moment of our lives is therefore to speak the name of God. This makes it our first and our last word as we enter and leave the world.

For some years now, I have taught this to contemplative groups in many countries, and it changes peoples' faith and prayer lives in substantial ways. I remind people that there is no Islamic, Christian, or Jewish way of breathing. There is no American, African, or Asian way of breathing. There is no rich or poor way of breathing. The playing field is utterly leveled. The air of the earth is one and the same air, and this divine wind "blows where it will" (John 3:8) — which appears to be everywhere. No one and no religion can control this spirit.

When considered in this way, God is suddenly as available and accessible as the very thing we all do constantly — breathe. Exactly as some teachers of prayer always said, "Stay with the breath, attend to your breath": the same breath that was breathed into Adam's nostrils by this Yahweh (Genesis 2:7); the very breath that Jesus handed over with trust on the cross (John 19:30) and then breathed on us as shalom, forgiveness, and the Holy Spirit all at once (John 20:21–23). And isn't it wonderful that breath, wind, spirit, and air are precisely *nothing* — and yet everything?

Just keep breathing consciously in this way and you will know that you are connected to humanity from cavemen to cosmonauts, to the entire animal world, and even to the trees and the plants. And we are now told that the atoms we breathe are physically the same as the stardust from the original Big Bang. Oneness is no longer merely a vague mystical notion, but a scientific fact.

CHAPTER THREE

Three Ways to View the Sunset

Three men stood by the ocean, looking at the same sunset.

One man saw the immense physical beauty and enjoyed the event in itself. This man was the "sensate" type who, like 80 percent of the world, deals with what he can see, feel, touch, move, and fix. This was enough reality for him, for he had little interest in larger ideas, intuitions, or the grand scheme of things. He saw with his first eye, which was good.

A second man saw the sunset. He enjoyed all the beauty that the first man did. Like all lovers of coherent thought, technology, and science, he also enjoyed his power to make sense of the universe and explain what he discovered. He thought about the cyclical rotations of planets and stars. Through imagination, intuition, and reason, he saw with his second eye, which was even better.

The third man saw the sunset, knowing and enjoying all that the first and the second men did. But in his ability to progress from seeing to explaining to "tasting," he also remained in awe before *an underlying mystery, coherence, and spaciousness* that connected him with everything else. He used his third eye, which is the full goal of all seeing and all knowing. This was the best.

THE URGENT NEED FOR CONTEMPLATIVE SEEING

Third-eye seeing is the way the mystics see. They do not reject the first eye; the senses matter to them, but they know there is more. Nor do they reject the second eye; but they know not to confuse knowledge with depth or mere correct information with the transformation of consciousness itself.[7] The mystical gaze builds upon the first two eyes — *and yet goes further.* It happens whenever, by some wondrous "coincidence," our heart space, our mind space, and our body awareness are all simultaneously open and nonresistant. I like to call it *presence.* It is experienced as a moment of deep inner connection, and it always pulls you, intensely satisfied, into the naked and undefended now, which can involve both profound joy and profound sadness. At that point, you either want to write poetry, pray, or be utterly silent.

In the early medieval period, two Christian philosophers at the monastery of St. Victor in Paris had names for these three ways of seeing, and these names had a great influence on scholars and seekers in the Western tradition. Hugh of St. Victor (1078–1141) and Richard of St. Victor (1123–1173) wrote that humanity was given three different sets of eyes, each building on the previous one. The first eye was the eye of the flesh (*thought* or *sight*), the second was the eye of reason (*meditation* or *reflection*), and the third eye was the eye of true understanding (*contemplation*).[8]

I cannot emphasize strongly enough that the separation and loss of these three necessary eyes is at the basis of much of the short-*sight*-edness and religious crises of the Western world. Lacking such wisdom, it is very difficult for churches, governments, and leaders to move beyond ego, the desire for control, and public posturing. Everything divides into oppositions such as liberal vs. conservative, with vested interests pulling against one another. Truth is no longer possible at this level of conversation. Even theology becomes more a quest for power than a search for God and Mystery.

One wonders how far spiritual and political leaders can genuinely lead us without some degree of mystical seeing and action. It is hardly an exaggeration to say that "us-and-them" seeing, and the dualistic thinking that results, is the foundation of almost all discontent and violence in the world.[9] It allows heads of religion and state to avoid their own founders, their own national ideals, and their own better instincts. Lacking the contemplative gaze, such leaders will remain mere functionaries and technicians, without any big picture to guide them for the long term. The world and the churches are filled with such people, often using God language as a cover for their own lack of certainty or depth.

The third-eye person has always been the saint, the seer, the poet, the metaphysician, or the authentic mystic who grasped the whole picture. There is more to the mystical gaze, however, than having "ecstatic visions." If people have ignored the first and the second eyes, their hold on the third eye is often temporary, shallow, and incapable of being shared with anybody else. We need true mystics who see with all three sets of eyes, not eccentrics, fanatics, or rebels. The true mystic is always both humble and compassionate, for she knows that she does not know.

WHAT IT MEANS TO BE A MYSTIC

Now do not let the word "mystic" scare you off. It simply means *one who has moved from mere belief systems or belonging systems to actual inner experience.* All spiritual traditions agree that such a movement is possible, desirable, and available to everyone. In fact, Jesus seems to say that this is the whole point! (See, for example, John 10:19–38.)

Some call this movement *conversion,* some call it *enlightenment,* some *transformation,* and some *holiness.* It is Paul's "third heaven," where he "heard things that must not and cannot be put into human language" (2 Corinthians 12:2, 4). Consciously or not, far too much organized religion has a vested interest in keeping you in the first or second heaven, where all can be put into proper language and deemed certain. This keeps you coming back to church, and it keeps us clergy in business.

This is not usually the result of ill will on anybody's part; it's just that you can lead people only as far as you yourself have gone. As we will see later, transformed people transform people. From the way they talk so glibly about what is always Mystery, it's clear that many clergy have never enjoyed the third heaven themselves, and they cannot teach what they do not know. Theological training without spiritual experience is deadly.

We are ready to see and taste the full sunset now and no longer need to prove it or even describe it. We just enjoy it — and much more!

CHAPTER FOUR

We Should Have "Known" Better

*Make no mistake about it — if any of you think of yourselves
as wise, you must learn to be ignorant first, and then you can
become wise.* — 1 CORINTHIANS 3:18

*How are we supposed to see one another as other Christs?
There is so much contrary evidence. Do we just pretend?*
— FROM A LETTER I RECEIVED

Recently I was watching a televised debate between advocates of
creationism or "Intelligent Design" and evolution. There were
educated people on both sides of the question, many in highly
professional positions. I kept waiting for someone to say, "This
is a bogus framing of the question" or "This does not need to
be a problem," but in the entire two hours, not a single person did! The two sides just continued to harden their positions
with well-argued language that broadly represented either a scientific worldview or a Creator-God worldview. They saw one
another as enemies; at times the conversation grew quite fiery,
and of course it went nowhere — nothing but defensive and
affronted minds.

I hoped for the scientists to open up to the possibility of the
central importance of mythic meanings for the soul, for sanity,
and for culture, but they kept beating one drum of facts and
information without reflecting on the context or the meaning

of those facts. I hoped for the religious people to take incarnation seriously and recognize the brilliance of a God who *creates things that keep creating themselves,* but they too kept beating one drum — of an extremely unimaginative and uninvolved God. It was all so sad, so futile, so unnecessary.

Both sides should have *known* better.

KNOWING WORSE:
ALL-OR-NOTHING THINKING

Watching the debaters deeply frustrated me, but honestly, I do the same. More than with any other personality trait in my life, all-or-nothing thinking has caused me to make huge mistakes and bad judgments, hurt people and myself, withhold love, and misinterpret situations. And this pattern of dualistic or polarity thinking is deeply entrenched in most Western people, despite its severe limitations. Binary thinking is not wrong or bad in itself — in fact, it is necessary in many if not most situations. But it is completely inadequate for the major questions and dilemmas of life.

Why do we do this to ourselves and one another? Don't I know that every viewpoint is a view from a point? Why can't I stand back and calmly observe that I always have a preference or bias or need, perhaps even a good and helpful one? Don't I know by now that some of the information is never all of the information? What is it that makes it so hard to backtrack from my position once I've declared it in my mind, and especially if I declare it publicly?

This ability to stand back and calmly observe my inner dramas, without rushing to judgment, is foundational for spiritual seeing. It is the primary form of "dying to the self" that Jesus lived personally and the Buddha taught experientially. The growing consensus is that, whatever you call it, *such calm, egoless seeing is invariably characteristic of people at the highest levels of doing and loving in all cultures and religions.* They are the ones we call sages or wise women or holy men. They see like the mystics see.

We have not been practically or systematically taught this higher-level seeing in the West, however, for some centuries now. That is a major theme in this book. The tragic results have been rationalism, secularism, and atheism on the Left and fundamentalism, tribal thinking, and cognitive rigidity on the Right. Neither is serving us well. This is why I question whether religion is doing its job. Fortunately, we still have the perennial and older tradition. With apologies to conservative Christians, this is the *much* older and more solid tradition, and from it we can again be taught.[10]

KNOWING BETTER: CONTEMPLATION AND PRESENCE

Today the unnecessary suffering on this earth is great for people who could have "known better" and should have been taught better by their religions. In the West, religion became preoccupied with *telling people what to know more than how to know, telling people what to see more than how to see.* We ended up seeing Holy Things faintly, trying to understand Great Things with a whittled-down mind, and trying to love God with our own small and divided heart. It has been like trying to view the galaxies with a $5 pair of binoculars.

As you will see, *contemplation,* my word for this larger seeing, keeps the whole field open; it remains vulnerable before the
moment, the event, or the person — before it divides and tries
to conquer or control it. Contemplatives refuse to create false
dichotomies, dividing the field for the sake of the quick comfort
of their ego. They do not rush to polarity thinking to take away
their mental anxiety. They are like Nicodemus (John 3:3 and
7:50) and Gamaliel (Acts 5:34–39, 22:3), well-trained Jewish
lawyers, solid in their own tradition, who were still willing to give
Jesus an opening and even respect, though the entire establish-
ment had made its final damning judgment. Jesus fit no current
or common definition of holiness in his time or within his group.
In their world, they were not rational or right-minded at all. On
some level, both Nicodemus and Gamaliel were contemplatives,
breaking through to nondual thinking.

I would like to call contemplation "full-access knowing" — not
irrational, but prerational, nonrational, rational, and transrational
all at once. Contemplation refuses to be reductionistic. Contemplation is an exercise in *keeping your heart and mind spaces open
long enough for the mind to see other hidden material.* It is content
with the naked now and waits for futures given by God and grace.
As such, a certain amount of love for an object and for myself
must precede any full knowing of it. As the Dalai Lama says so
insightfully, "A change of heart is always a change of mind." You
could say the reverse as well — a change of mind is also a change
of heart. Eventually they *both* must change for us to see properly.

Western Judeo-Christians are often uncomfortable with the
word "nonduality." They often associate it (negatively) with Eastern religions. I am convinced, however, that *Jesus was the first
nondual religious teacher of the West,* and one reason we have

failed to understand so much of his teaching, much less follow it, is because we tried to understand it with a dualistic mind.[11] That will be another major theme in this book, but I will have to clear away the debris from many sides so that instead of taking my word for it, you can see it for yourself.

This brilliant word, nonduality (*advaita* in Sanskrit), was used by many in different traditions in the East to distinguish from total and perfect absorption or enmeshment. Facing some of the same challenges of modern-day ecology and quantum physics, they did not want to say that all things were metaphysically or physically identical, nor did they want to separate and disconnect everything. In effect, the contemplative mind in East or West withholds from labeling things or categorizing them too quickly, so it can come to see them in themselves, apart from the words or concepts that become their substitutes.

Humans tend to think that because they agree or disagree with the idea of a thing, they have realistically encountered the thing itself. Not at all true, says the contemplative. It is necessary to encounter the thing in itself. "Presence" is my word for this encounter, a different way of knowing and touching the moment. It is much more vulnerable, and leaves us without a sense of control. Thomas had his *idea* of Jesus, but had to trustfully put his finger into his side before he could "know" the truth (John 20:27). Such panoramic and deeper seeing requires a lot of practice, but the rewards are superb and, I believe, necessary for both joy and truth in this world.

The fact that nonpolarity thinking is at the core of three of the world's greatest religions — Hinduism, Buddhism, and Taoism — demands that we give it at least a "Gamaliel hearing." I will try to demonstrate that although we did not use the precise word "nondual," the idea was consistently *assumed, implied, and even taught* in Christianity for at least sixteen hundred years. It then largely went underground for a number of reasons, as we will try to show here and later in the book.

MYSTICAL CHRISTIANITY: A CRITIQUE FROM WITHIN

I have often wondered how we could have lost such vast wisdom from the ages. I expect no more from the systems of power, which need to be dualistic in order to survive. But unfortunately, organized religion today too often offers easy and false dichotomies to its own mass membership. Whether popes, patriarchs, mullahs, rabbis, imams, bishops, or clerics, many who should be elders and teachers, and should know better from their own study and prayer, seem to be strongly invested in either-or thinking. It gives them a sense of certitude, clear authority, and control over all the confusing data. Once you must speak for any group, a whole set of biases necessarily come into play. It has little to do with bad intentions on the part of individuals. Protocols, procedures, policies, consistency, hiring and firing, communion and excommunication — all become quite necessary, it seems. At this level, we all become invested in what Wallace Stevens called "a blessed rage for order," even though our founder, Jesus, seemed quite comfortable with the constant disorder of his world. How do we reconcile these two? Is it even possible?

A large percentage of religious people become and remain quite rigid thinkers because their religion taught them that to be faithful, obedient, and stalwart in the ways of God, they had to create order. They too are not bad people; they simply never learned much about wisdom, paradox, or mystery as the very nature of faith. When so many become professional church workers without going through spiritual transformation at any deep level, religious work becomes a career, and church becomes something one "attends." Real transformation is not called for or even desired.[12] This has been going on for centuries, and in all religions.

Throughout history, contemplative seeing appears to be the minority position, which is probably what Jesus is so disappointed with in the Judaism of his time. Many of the folks in Jesus' time, particularly the leaders, simply cannot see what he sees (e.g., Matthew 13:13ff.). It has nothing to do with his being the "Son of God" or having special access to truth, *or he would not be able to find the religious leaders culpable.* He keeps saying, in effect, "You all should know better. You do not know your own wonderful Jewish tradition."

Like any true reformer or prophet, Jesus critiques Judaism from within, by its own criteria and its own documents.[13] This is what I hope to do here for Christianity or any religion. Too often, religion offers more doctrinal conclusions, more competing truth claims in the increasingly large marketplace of religious claims, but seldom does it give people a vision, process, and practices whereby they can legitimate those truth claims for themselves — by inner experience and actual practices.

In my own Catholic tradition, the official church has invariably kept mystics, hermits, charismatic types, and "prayer people" at arms' length — at least until they have been dead for a hundred years and can be sanitized. I understand this, because their experiences usually cannot be packaged for mass consumption. In fact, I am convinced that most of the major beliefs and doctrines of the Christian churches can be understood, relished, and effectively lived only by nondual consciousness, by contemplatives, by people who know how to be *present* to the naked and broad now (e.g., Jesus is "fully human and fully divine," Mary is both virgin and mother, bread is still bread and yet Jesus, etc.). They alone know deeply and include widely. As Karl Rahner is often quoted as saying, "The devout Christian of the future will either be a 'mystic'... or he will cease to be anything at all."

The great mystics of every tradition invite us to *know better*, to draw from the resources of our own tradition and see in a way that honors debate, reason, and order while also moving beyond them. Can we answer the mystics' invitation? Can we begin to attain the mystical gaze Rahner suggests we must? I think we are on the very edge of history — and about to be edged over — by the depth of the need and from the depths of our own desire.

CHAPTER FIVE

A Lesson from the Monks

Do not plunder the Mystery with concepts.
— ZEN MASTERS

My religion is kindness.
— THE DALAI LAMA

What is the goal of religions? What do they equip us to learn, see, or become? As I study the history and teachings of the world religions, I am deeply struck by one overwhelming difference. In Native religions and in the religions of the East, one consistently finds the goal to be "harmony," the overcoming of distinctions, conflicts, and oppositional energy by various conversions of the mind, the heart, the emotions, the body, and the will. They tend to be less concerned about metaphysics than we are, and also less concerned about the next world. We have different gifts, and also overlapping strengths.

Most ancient teachings — including those of Jesus and the Desert Fathers and Mothers, as well as aphorisms, riddles, stories, wisdom sayings, and concrete practices — revealed the small self to the person and opened her up to some form of the divine self. These wise teachings invariably sought to create balance both within and without. The emphasis was on spiritual practice — and on *practices* much more than on believing cerebral ideas to be true or false. They did not worry about "sin management" the way we Western clergy did. Their concern was usually to seek some kind of equilibrium, inner harmony, or peace, which took many different forms and emphases. In general, they thought that *balance brought one to divine union more than moral perfection did.* It is very hard for Westerners to make this switch — to most of us it feels soft and amorphous.

THE LIMITATIONS OF INDIVIDUALISM

For some reason, monotheistic religions think that deciding who is going where and why — Catholics add "when" — is our business. Perhaps we think it is the only way to have some control over people, society, and the future. Muslims are damning Christians to hell, Christians are telling Jews they are not saved, and Jews, for example, spat at me when I joined them praying at the Wailing Wall wearing my Franciscan habit. How did we ever come to this in the name of such a loving God?

The monotheistic religions that emerged in the West largely took on the organizational model and the verbal debate forms of the West. In our style of debate, you either win or lose, make points or lose points. Religiously, you are either saved or unsaved, in or out of grace. We like clarity and we like strong identity, which is good as far as it goes. Monotheism seems to have both that strength and that weakness. It wants to hold everything together inside its one God and its one rather clear explanation. Europe preferred a notion of Christendom to actual community. This choice for clear identity made the West a highly dynamic civilization on many levels, and this was not entirely for the worse.

Native and Eastern peoples had teachers and wise people as well, but there did not tend to be any centralized control of the message by book, role, or office. The people went to the medicine men, the shamans, the hermits, the enlightened ones, the gurus, the ceremonies, the temples, the rituals — and, in my opinion, produced at least as high a rate of transformed people as the West did. When I travel, I surely see as many of the gifts of the Spirit (Galatians 5:22) among non-Christians as Christians, and often even more. In fact, in much of the world temples see a continual flow of people all day, every day, whereas many of ours are closed except for Sunday mornings or Sabbath services.

Judaism, Christianity, and Islam have not been known for creating "harmonizing" people. In general, peacemaking, nonviolence, love for the outsider or the poor, humility, and dialogue have never been the strength of these religions. Even though many people in each group attained higher levels of transformation, our concern was usually group order, consistency, organization, and clarifying and enforcing of membership requirements: not all bad, but not all good either, because we lost some essential values that the harmony-based religions preserved. (Members of those religions could probably identify values they lost as well.)

The fact that the two great wars emerged in a Christian Europe filled with churches and theology schools needs to be examined. The fact that racism, profound social inequity, and anti-Semitism were not broadly recognized as a serious problem until almost two thousand years after Jesus is forever a judgment on the immaturity of Western Christianity, whether Catholic or Protestant. Communism often emerged in formerly Christian cultures where social injustice had not been addressed in any serious way (China being the major exception). The former colonies of Latin America have never been known for even minimal social justice since their inception, despite their Catholic identity. The genocide of American Indians and the enslavement of black Africans seems not to have been a problem for North American Protestants. Sexism did not begin to be seriously faced until after the 1950s, and its remedies are still ignored and even resisted by most patriarchal churches. Elitism, classism, torture, homophobia, poverty, and the degradation of the earth are still largely unaddressed by the ordinary monotheistic "believer." Such issues do not count in most salvation theories. I list all these not to be negative, but to let us see the very real limitations of the overdefining and over-asserting of the individual self and its private salvation — and the expansion of that false self into ideas such as "my Christian country." The individual became "individuated" in the West, without any keen awareness of the common good or the harmonizing of body, mind, heart, and community. That highly individuated personality colonized the world and spread its conquering version of Christianity.

"Catholic" means universal (Greek *kata-holon:* according to the whole). Yet in my experience, most Roman and Anglican Catholics, and most Orthodox, are much more provincial and ethnic than truly universal. And most Protestants are still protesting too much rather than transforming themselves or their cultures. In both individualistic groups, there has never been much concern for social sin or institutional evil. Spirituality lost out, and now so many of our people go elsewhere to find what they seek: support groups, conferences, books, or do-it-yourself plans. According to a recent national study, 44 percent of Americans today are somewhere else than in the church of their upbringing. The second biggest "denomination" after Roman Catholics is *former* Roman Catholics. Has this ever happened before in history? One wonders if a civilization can flourish when so many of its people are so alienated from their own tradition and religion.

A DEBATE EVERYONE CAN WIN

Here is a true story that might illustrate what others have to teach us. Perhaps it can invite us Westerners out of our left brains and into our "other hemisphere." A friend of mine, Thomas Williams, once brought back a stack of photos from a monastery he visited in Tibet. Older and younger monks were pictured in what was called, in our translation, the "consequentalist debate." In every photo there was a young monk seated on the ground and an older one seemingly circling around him. In many of the pictures, one or both of them was smiling or gesturing.

He told me that during the young novice's training, he or she is presented over a period of three years with each and every one of the Buddha's teachings. During that time, she has to name all of the difficult and problematic consequences that would follow from observing this teaching. After each answer, the older monks clap their hands in approval, and they smile at one another. When all of the possible negative consequences are exhausted, they move onto the good consequences. The same procedure is followed until all of the good consequences have been unpacked, no matter how many hours or days it takes. And again, after each answer, the masters clap their hands, and they smile at one another.

It appears to be patient and disciplined training in nonpolarity thinking and in broader reflection and discrimination. There is no declaration of the perfect answer or the wrong answer. The novice is quite simply being taught how to weigh and discern, see and understand the good and bad consequences — and from that open field, to learn himself and learn how to wisely advise others. What an utterly different structure compared to a Western debate style! With us, one must win and the other must lose. (This is our style of religion, too.)

Here is the clincher. *The only way you can lose the consequentalist debate is to stop smiling!* Obviously, this calls for a letting go of the ego. Have you ever noticed that in any situation, when your ego is invested, afraid, or needy, it's very hard to smile? But when the truth is not your personal possession, it is very easy to smile.

The concern in Tibetan Buddhism is not to achieve a conceptually perfect answer, which then has to be defended, but to call forth a happy, loving, aware, and perceptive human being. Is that not one type of "salvation"? The impulse behind this worldview is reflected in the wider society. Tibet is one of the very few wisdom-based cultures left in the world, and despite enormous pressures it has never been warlike or aggressive. Jesus would probably feel at home there.

Many of us have heard Dr. Phil, the TV therapist, tell couples in counseling that sooner or later every married person has to decide "Do I want to be right, or do I want to be happy?" He says he is saddened and surprised at how many prefer to be right — and therefore are seldom happy. He then adds to their shock with his signature question, "And how is that working for you?"

At this point in human and Western history, we have to ask that same question. "Christianity, how is this working for you?" Remember, Jesus never said, "This is my commandment: thou shalt be right." But that is the only way that both the ego and the dualistic mind know how to frame reality. It is not working.

It is an amazing arrogance that allows Christians to so readily believe that their mental understanding of things is anywhere close to that of Jesus. Jesus said, "I am the Way, the Truth, and the Life" (John 14:6). I think the intended effect of that often misused line is this: If Jesus is the Truth, then you probably aren't!

CHAPTER SIX

Glimpses of Wonder

The Quest Is Begun

[Mary] was deeply disturbed [by the words of the angel] and wondered what they might mean. — LUKE 1:29

[The disciples in meeting the risen Jesus] were so in wonder that they could not believe it. — LUKE 24:41

"Wondering" is a word connoting at least three things:

> Standing in disbelief
>
> Standing in the question itself
>
> Standing in awe before something

Try letting all three "standings" remain open inside of you. This is a very good way to grow spiritually, as long as the disbelief moves beyond mere skepticism or negativity.

When Scholastic philosophy was at its best (in the twelfth and thirteenth centuries), the development of an idea proceeded by what the great teachers called the *questio* (Latin, "to seek"). Our English word "quest" may come from that understanding. Like the monastic practice we saw in the previous chapter, the systematic asking of questions opened up wonder and encouraged spiritual curiosity by drawing out pros and cons for answers to the question, thus refining the question itself instead of just looking for the perfect answer.

At that time, Franciscans and Dominicans were like a Catholic debating society, hardly ever holding the same exact opinion, and in those days both of us could remain inside the Catholic fold. Unfortunately, in later centuries this practice degenerated to just needing answers. And preferably certain answers. And preferably about everything. We moved from wondering to answering, which has not served us well at all. This reached its nadir in what we today call fundamentalism, common in almost all religions. Let's start wondering again, in the way I describe above:

I have wondered why the major religions rarely produce many active peacemakers.

I have wondered why atheism is most common in Christian and Western cultures, and why formerly religious people are often the most anti-religious.

I have wondered why many people close down any threatening discussion by searching quickly for a single "but." (It has been demonstrated that a journalist only has to quote one opposing source, and people will use that to dismiss or doubt anything they don't want to hear.)

I have wondered why political thinking is so jingoistic and seems little able to work toward consensus or the common good.

I have wondered why the reasons for most wars in history — reasons that seemed so compelling at the time — look foolish, wrong, or often naïve to later generations.

Perhaps you have asked yourself similar questions: Why do people become so attached to political parties and habits of thought that they even vote against their own self-interest and cherished beliefs? Why do so many people have a clearer idea of what they are against that what they are for? You might wonder why, in politics, we call people "strong" simply because they never change their mind. You wonder why the same story line of good guys and bad guys is the narrative of most movies, novels, operas, and theater. You wonder why people who hate religion tend to attack it with the same dogmatism that they hate in religion.

If you've ever wondered about questions like these, I invite you to sit with your "wonder." Instead of letting your disbelief harden into skepticism or negativity, let yourself wonder — feel awe in the presence of — these insights into the way all of us think. What does this duality teach us about the human condition? What can it teach you about yourself?

CHAPTER SEVEN

But We Have to Make Judgments, Don't We?

With him it was always "Yes!"
— PAUL, SPEAKING OF JESUS
IN 2 CORINTHIANS 1:19

Almost all spiritual teachers say something to this effect: "Do not judge." There is Jesus in Matthew 7:1 and Luke 6:36–38; there is the Buddha in the *Dhammapada,* 4:7. *Do not judge.* This may seem like a naïve, impossible, and even dangerous command. At conferences people will often say to me, "But we have to make judgments! We can't just walk around all day saying 'It's all good.' Sometimes you have to draw the line." Of course, they are right. But the great teachers aren't asking us to turn off our common sense and our rational minds; they are pointing to something deeper. So we need to discover what the heart of this teaching is.

WE SEE WHAT WE ARE READY TO SEE

The great teachers are saying that you cannot start seeing or understanding anything if you start with "No." You have to start with a "Yes" of basic acceptance, which means not too quickly labeling, analyzing, or categorizing things in or out, good or bad. You have to leave the field open. The ego seems to strengthen itself by constriction, by being against, or by re-action, and it feels loss or fear when it opens up. Spiritual teachers want you to live by positive action, open field, and conscious understanding, and not by resistance, knee-jerk reactions, or defensiveness. This is not easy: it often takes a lifetime of work and honest self-observation to stop judging or starting with "no."

Philosophically and psychologically, a certain *assent* precedes all true knowing. If you watch closely, you will often see that an initial change of heart or attitude precedes any willingness to change your mind. In my own Franciscan philosophical tradition, both St. Bonaventure and John Duns Scotus taught that love or willingness were higher than mere knowledge. You really know only that which you first love, they felt, because otherwise you invariably distort and divide your sight and eliminate any bothersome or threatening information. Then you do not love *it* but (at best) only your *idea* of it. How often we see this in our relationships: romance instead of real love, and infatuation ("false fire" in Latin) instead of genuine fire. Words and thoughts are invariably dualistic, but *pure experience is always nondualistic.* Think about that!

Fundamentalism suffers from the same false seeing. It is basically a love affair with words and ideas about God instead of God himself or herself. But you cannot really love words; you can only think them. You cannot really love reality with the judgmental mind, because you'll always try to control it, fix it, or understand it before you give yourself to it. And usually it is never fixed enough to deserve your protected gift of self. So you stay on Delay, Stall, or Pause forever. We see this fear of intimacy in most people, but in particular with men, who tend to have a more defended ego structure.

The fact that some form of loving must precede true knowing helps us appreciate why the prophets used the intimate word for carnal knowledge or sexual intimacy when they spoke of "knowing" God (see, for example, Hosea 2:21, 6:6, and John 10:14–15, 14:20, 17:3). This is a tremendous insight, but one that comes only from inner realization and not from books. So many of the mystics and the Song of Songs had to make use of sexual images to describe the relationship of the soul with God. From inside experience, you know God's love is a tender dance of give-and-take, rescue and holding.

We see what we are ready to see, expect to see, and even desire to see. There is some kind of mutual influence between subject and object, says the Heisenberg Principle — so much so that researchers in the medical world have to use placebos and "double blinds" to guarantee the results of their studies, and this is true equally among educated and uneducated subjects. Who would have thought the effect was so profound? Some who do not expect to get sick, don't; and some who do, do! Thus, you must never start with the negative or begin with an attitude of "no." If you start with no, you usually get some form of no back. If you start with yes, you are much more likely to get a yes back. It could be called Nonviolence Class 101.

Once you have learned to say a fundamental yes, later no's can be helpful and even necessary: without them, you have no protected boundaries or identity. Our modern world has coined a word for people who cannot say no: "co-dependents." No one ever taught them how and when to protect themselves with a necessary no, and that a no can be just as sacred as a yes. The value of no was in fact probably the import of so much teaching about the "avoidance of sin." Learning to say no to yourself gives you a sense of boundary and identity in the first half of life, but too many people make it an end in itself and then, by the second half of life, became highly judgmental. Such forms of religion end up obsessed with purity codes rather than compassion, justice, and a clean heart.

Never underestimate the absolute importance — and the difficulty — of starting each encounter with a primal "yes!" Isn't this what we consistently see in great people and those who make a difference? To start each encounter with "no" is largely what it means to be unconscious or unaware. You eventually become so *defended* that you cannot love or see well, and so *defensive* that you cannot change. This is a form of blindness that often passes for intelligence, prudence, or even *good "judgment."* Negating personalities often "hide behind the thickets of the law," as Robert Bolt recognized in the enemies of St. Thomas More. For some unfortunate reason, complaining, rejecting, or fearing something strengthens your sense of ego and makes you feel like you are important. You contract back into your small and false self, and from there, unfortunately, it becomes harder and harder to reemerge.

THE RADICAL PERCEPTUAL SHIFT: IS IT TRUE?

In all situations, of course, the all-important question is: *"Is it true?"* Not: "Is it from my group?" "Does it please me?" "Does it displease me?" "Does it use my vocabulary and my definitions?" Not even "Is it 100 percent true?" Who cares? the saint would say. "Only the ego cares," the Buddhist would say; and the ego is not interested in truth or in God, only in control. If it is even 10 percent true, the saint is grateful and happy for that gift.

St. Thomas Aquinas said in the thirteenth century: If it is true, then it is from the Holy Spirit. In the thirteenth century, when Christians demonized Muslims even more than they do today, St. Francis told us friars that if we found a page of the Koran, we should kiss it and place it on the altar. His Christian truth was not fear-based. He could honor God and holiness anywhere it was found, and not just inside of his own symbol system.[14]

If there is indeed one God of all the earth, then it is this one God who is breaking through in every age and culture, and monotheists should be the first to recognize that truth is one (Ephesians 4:4–6) and that God is "all in all" (1 Corinthians 15:28). Yet they usually end up fearing and even opposing these ideas, probably because in their own lives their religion has been tribal more than transformative. Perhaps we want to belong to something exclusive, the equivalent of a religious country club, but by that time, of course, our God has become very small and been whittled down to our size. As Rumi said, "There are a thousand ways to kneel and kiss the ground."

◆ Most writers in the early Christian era called this radical perceptual shift away from the judging and separate self *contemplation*.

◆ Buddhists called it meditation, sitting, or practicing.

◆ Hesychastic Orthodoxy called it prayer of the heart.

◆ Sufi Islam called it ecstasy.

◆ Hasidic Judaism called it living from "the divine spark within."

◆ Vedantic Hinduism (the earliest) spoke of it as nondual knowing or simply breathing.

◆ Native religions found it in communion with nature itself or the Great Spirit through dance, ritual, and sexuality: "original participation," as Owen Barfield called it.[15]

Presence is experienced in a participative way, outside the mind. The mind by nature is intent on judging, controlling, and analyzing instead of seeing, tasting, and loving. This is exactly why it *cannot* be present or live in the naked now. The mind wants a job and loves to process things. The key to stopping this game is, quite simply, peace, silence, or stillness. This was always seen as God's primary language, "with everything else being a very poor translation," as Fr. Thomas Keating wisely observes. I would even say that *on the practical level, silence and God will be experienced simultaneously — and even as the same thing.* And afterward, you will want to remain even more silent. The overly verbal religion of the last five hundred years does not seem to understand this at all and tends to be afraid of any silence whatsoever. It cannot follow Jesus and go into the desert for forty days, where there is nothing to say, to prove, to think, or to defend.

Although we all use the phrase "peace of mind," there is really no such thing. When you are in your mind, you are never truly at peace, and when you are truly at peace, you are never in your mind. Don't *believe or disbelieve that statement either, just honestly observe yourself. Then you will know* — but it will be an altogether new kind of knowing.

CHAPTER EIGHT

Yes, But

Yes, the mind is necessary, but it can't do everything.

Yes, the mind is receptive, but reason is not our only antenna. We also need our bodies, our emotions, our hearts, our nose, our ears, our eyes, our taste, and our souls.

Yes, the mind can achieve great things, but through overcontrol, it can also limit what we can know.

Yes, the mind can think great thoughts, and also bad and limiting ones. The mind can be a gift and a curse.

Yes, the mind can tell left from right, but it cannot perceive invisible things such as love, eternity, fear, wholeness, mystery, or the Divine.

Yes, the mind can discern consistency, logic, and fairness, but it seldom puts these into practice.

Yes, the mind and reason are necessary, but they must learn to distinguish between what lies beyond its reach: the prerational and the transrational.

Yes, the mind is brilliant, but the more we observe it, the more we see it is also obsessive and repetitive.

Yes, the mind seeks the truth, but it can also create lies.

Yes, the mind can connect us with others, but it can also keep us apart.

Yes, the mind is very useful, but when it does not recognize its own finite viewpoint, it is also useless.

Yes, the mind can serve the world, but in fact it largely serves itself.

Yes, the mind can make necessary distinctions, but it also divides in thought what is undivided in nature and in the concrete.

Yes, the mind is needed, but we also need other ways of knowing or we will not know well, fully, or freely.

Yes, the mind is good at thinking. But so much so that most humans, like Descartes, think they *are* their thinking.

Yes, the mind likes to think, but until it learns to listen to others, to the body, the heart, and all the senses, it also uses itself to block everything it does not like to do or to acknowledge.

Yes, the mind is our friend, but when we are obsessive or compulsive, it can also be our most dangerous foe.

Yes, the mind welcomes education, but it also needs to be *uneducated,* to learn how much of what it "knows" is actually mere conditioning and prejudice.

As a result, the great religions of the world found methods to compartmentalize, but not eliminate, the overcontrol of the thinking, rational mind, through practices such as prayer, meditation, or contemplation. This was the "new mind," which allowed

1. other parts of us to *see,*

2. other things to *be seen,*

3. the rational mind to then be reintegrated, but now *as a servant instead of the master.*

I risk the criticism that "It can't be that simple." But it really is almost that simple — yet, for some reason, very hard to do.

CHAPTER NINE

Not Many Things, but One Thing

*Martha, Martha, you worry about the ten thousand
  things.*
So few are needed,
Indeed only one. — A PARAPHRASE OF LUKE 10:42

These well-known words come from Jesus to his dear friend,
Martha. He is the house guest of Mary, Martha, and Lazarus.
Martha is doing the reasonable, hospitable thing, the one expected of her gender — rushing around, fixing, preparing, and
as the text brilliantly says, "distracted with all the serving."

Martha was everything good and right, but one thing she was
not. She was not *present* — most likely, not present to herself,
her own feelings of resentment, perhaps her own martyr com-
plex, her need to be needed. This is the kind of goodness that
does no good! If she was not present to herself, she could not
truly be present to her guests in any healing way, and spiritually speaking, she could not even be present to God. Presence is
presence is presence. How you do it is how you do everything.
Jesus challenged her at the daily, ordinary, human level because
that would reflect her same pattern at the divine level. For her,
this was indeed "the one thing necessary." So much of religion
involves teaching people this and that, an accumulation of facts

and imperatives that is somehow supposed to add up to salvation. The great teachers know that one major change is needed: *how we do the moment.* Then all the this-and-thats will fall into line. This is true! This is so important that Jesus was willing to challenge and upset his hostess and make use of a teachable moment — in the very moment.

Jesus affirms Mary precisely in this way: how she is doing the moment. She knows how to be present to him and, presumably, to herself. She understands the one thing that makes all other things happen at a deeper and healing level.

What is true for Mary and Martha is true for us as well. "Only one thing is necessary," Jesus says. If you are present, you will eventually and always experience the Presence. It is so simple, and so hard to teach. To people who have never experienced it, it can even sound like a cheap affirmation. I urge the Martha in all of us: please do not make that mistake.

GETTING THROWN OFF YOUR HORSE: SUDDEN CONVERSION

Knowledge is the gathering of information. It consists in knowing about "the ten thousand things," as the Buddhists poetically call it. It involves "having the facts straight." This is beneficial to have. But all the information in the world does not of itself accumulate into wisdom.[16] In fact, as the Franciscan St. Bonaventure noted, "Wisdom is confusing to the proud and often evident to the lowly."[17]

Wisdom is not the gathering of more facts and information, as if that would eventually coalesce into truth. *Wisdom is precisely a different way of seeing and knowing those ten thousand things.*

I suggest that *wisdom is precisely the freedom to be present.* Wise people always know how to be present, but it is much more than that. Presence *is* wisdom! People who are fully present know how to see fully, rightly, and truthfully. Presence is the one thing necessary, and in many ways, the hardest thing of all. Just try to keep your heart open, your mind without division or resistance, and your body not somewhere else. Presence is the practical, daily task of all mature religion and all spiritual disciplines.

If you observe wise people, you see that they actually lose a certain interest in gathering more and more information, books, and news. These can clutter what is already a clear field, open sight, and simple presence to the moment. When I return from my Lenten hermitage, for about two or three months I have no interest in reading, and then I slowly fall back into it. We already know far more than Jesus or Buddha ever knew, but the great difference is that *they knew what they did know from a different level and in a different way.* The same powerful Scripture text that brings a loving person to even greater love will be mangled and misused by a fearful or egocentric person.

This is surely what Jesus means when he talks about the one who *has* being given more and those who *have not* losing what little they have (Matthew 13:12). Once your presence is right, you grow from everything, even the problematic. If your presence is wrong, you will not even recognize the Real Presence when it shows itself every day. The Presence will be there — it always is — but *you* won't be.

Proof of this can be seen even in Jesus' own life. Most of Jesus' contemporaries missed the "Real Presence" that was right in their midst, and most of them were religiously observant people or, as we might say today, "practicing Catholics." They were looking for religion, and he was just a human being. They were storing up treasures for the next world, and he was just living and talking about what was right in front of him — birds, lilies, tenants, and suffering. Eternity is going on all the time, and spiritual teachers gave us a way to dip into that stream now and therefore forever. Their assumption is invariably, "If you have it now, you will have it then." They see a perfect continuity between time and eternity. This is why they do not fear death or judgment. If God loves me so unconditionally now, why would God change the love policy later?

I have often been puzzled by the common view that conversion is a one-time event. This view does not match my observation of myself or others. Yet such conversion is described in so many stories from all of the world religions. Finally, it became clearer to me what the stories were trying to say. When your "program" changes, you will indeed speak of your conversion as a momentary event, something that happens in an instant. But if you examine the accounts of peoples' great moments of breakthrough, they usually are not referring to *what they see* as much as *how they see.* Such renewed sight is indeed like being *born again* — "once I was blind, and now I see." Even though St. Paul's conversion as described in the New Testament never mentions a horse, we often speak of his conversion as "being thrown off a horse on the Damascus road." That's what true conversion feels like.

Are you ready to be thrown off your own horse?

GRADUAL CONVERSION

True and full conversion (head, heart, gut) does not really happen until the new program is in the hard-wiring and becomes a permanent and "natural" trait rather than a one-time emotion. This process takes most of one's life, and is actually the very task of life and of contemplation. This difference partially explains the widespread disillusionment with people today who claim to be religiously converted. Many seem to have some kind of genuine spiritual breakthrough but never get around to the intellectual, lifestyle, and ethical implications that often take years to recognize and integrate. (We will talk more about this in chapter 11.)

One increasing consensus among scholars and spiritual observers is that this conversion or enlightenment moves forward step by step from almost totally dualistic thinking to nondual thinking at the highest levels.[18] This matches my own experience, study, and observation. We call that higher way of seeing and being present *contemplation*. If this ancient gift could be clarified and recovered for Western Christians, Muslims, and Jews, religion would experience a monumental leap forward. We could start *being present to one another.* We could live in the naked now instead of hiding in the past or worrying about the future, as we mentally rehearse resentments and make our case for why we are right and someone else is wrong.

Throughout this book I talk about the "one thing" — not to give you my conclusions, but to invite you to try on a new pair of glasses and to keep your lens clean. Then you will come to some excellent conclusions for yourself. I can truly trust that. Just learn how to see, and you will know whatever it is that you need to see. When I first began my degree in philosophy decades ago, we started with a boring and abstract course called *epistemology.* It did not tell us what to know, *metaphysics,* but how we know what we think we know. Little did I appreciate how wise my friar teachers were! Too many clergy study religion and Scripture before they critique their own lens and process. They see without examining their way of seeing.

Good religion, however, is always about *seeing* rightly: "The lamp of the body is the eye; if your eye is sound, your whole body will be filled with light," as Jesus says in Matthew 6:22. *How you see is what you see.* And to see rightly is to be able to be fully present — without fear, without bias, and without judgment. It is such hard work for the ego, for the emotions, and for the body, that I think most of us would simply prefer to go to church services.

We will note in the last chapter how this differs from what Oprah Winfrey and others call the "Law of Attraction" and the "Secret," but in fact, this wisdom *has* been kept a huge secret, even though Jesus, perhaps Moses, and surely Buddha taught it to their followers. We'll look at what was lost, how it was lost, and how we can still retrieve the *real* secret. Moses could never have seen burning bushes as the Divine, could never have persevered with so much unknowing, unless he had moved to a higher level of seeing.

HOW MARTHA BECOMES MARY: WILLFULNESS AND WILLINGNESS

There is only one catch, but it's a big one. You cannot just try on this pair of glasses as if you were at LensCrafters. Without exception, all of the wisdom traditions would insist that this wisdom is given and not taken, waited for and not demanded, having much more to do with long-term willingness than mere willfulness.[19] This is the *undergoing* we noted earlier.

This willingness comes at a price and invariably demands that you pass through some rings of fire, which most of us would rather not do. There are few teachers of the dark path, the journey through the shadowlands, the actual way of the cross. And most organized religion in the West has emphasized will power (heroic ego-affirming virtues) rather than willingness, which seldom affirms the ego. So most of us idealize willfulness. I recently read that 80 percent of American soldiers divorce after they have an autistic or severely handicapped child. We are trained to be strong against strength, but we are usually weak and afraid in dealing with "weakness."

The need for willingness is counterintuitive for almost all Western people, especially the strong and the educated, who think that spiritual things can be achieved by intellect and will power. In fact, it will demand a severe detachment from what you think is your intellect, and you cannot get there by trying harder. This is a difficult lesson for most people, which is probably why Jesus called it the "narrow path that few would walk upon" (Matthew 7:14).

All great spirituality is somehow about letting go. Trust me on this crucial point. As we'll see later, there are two paths that break down our dualistic thinking and our inability to let go: the path of great love and the path of great suffering. Neither of them can be willed, truly understood, or programmed by any method whatsoever. There is no precise technique or foolproof formula for love or suffering. They are their own teachers, the best of teachers, in their own time and in their unique way each time. If you are like me, however, you would rather have teaching in the head than what I call "the authority of those who have suffered" and have emerged from the belly of the whale, transformed.

Here we are in the hands of fate, destiny, God, Providence, and grace. The paradox is that wisdom and full presence is always given as a gift, and you only know the gift *after* having passed through the belly of the whale. Jesus said in Luke 11:29 that this "sign of Jonah" was the only sign he would ever give; considering all the signs religious people seek, this is quite a remarkable claim!

There is an old saying that "no one catches the wild ass by running, and yet only those who run ever catch the wild ass." Maybe we can say, "No one comes to God just by loving or suffering, yet only those who have loved and suffered seem to come to God more deeply." Martha never gets there by being more of Martha, and yet Martha's running, distraction, and clumsy, futile attempts at love are the beginning of her eventual transformation into Mary. It is the same for all of us.

PART TWO

CHAPTER TEN

What about Jesus?

Tell all the Truth but tell it slant...

Too bright for our infirm Delight
The Truth's superb surprise!

The Truth must dazzle gradually
Or every man be blind.

— EMILY DICKINSON

The sayings of Jesus are among the most beloved of all words in our world today. How, then, did people lose sight of his nondual message? We will look at part of the problem in our reflection on "the lost tradition" later. For all practical purposes, the dualistic mind is not able to accept the orthodox teaching from the Council of Nicea that Jesus is both fully human and fully divine at the same time. It does not compute with our computer! Our dualistic mind needs to split and divide, with the result that it understands Jesus as *only* divine and understands human beings as *only* human, despite all scriptural and mystical affirmations to the contrary. The overcoming of this divide was the whole point of the Incarnation of God in Christ. The results for Christianity, and for individual Christians, have been truly disastrous.

While entire books could be written on the topic of Jesus as the first nondual thinker in the West (Cynthia Bourgeault's *The Wisdom Jesus* is one recent excellent example), here I want to give you a sampling of the vast evidence for Jesus' contemplative teaching. As we'll see, some of his most provocative sayings make much more sense when read nondually and in many cases are incomprehensible in any other way.

◆ ◆ ◆

The manifestation of the Great I AM in Jesus, which was the momentous Christian epiphany, became so thrilling to the new era that they forgot the continued need to balance his newly discovered divinity with his personally and even more strongly proclaimed humanity. Remember, virtually Jesus' only form of self-reference — eighty-seven times among the four Gospels — was *ben' adam,* a son of the human one.[20] There was no capitalization in the Hebrew texts of the Bible, so the would-be formal title "Son of Man," drawn from an obscure passage in Daniel, is, I believe, unwarranted and unfounded. Jesus is in fact emphasizing "I am like you" — a mortal, a human, everyman! This is how the same phrase is used ninety-three times by Ezekiel. Why do we need to read it differently in the mouth of Jesus?

Our preoccupation with his divinity did not allow us to hear about his own proudly proclaimed and clearly emphasized humanity. In practice, most of the Christian era has been guilty of a heresy that it formally condemned. We often think of Jesus as having *only* a divine nature, and this misses and avoids the major point he came to bring. We were not able to balance humanity and divinity in Jesus, which probably reflects why we were unable to put it together in ourselves. We did not have the proper software for the task. Theism believes there is a God. *Christianity believes that God and humanity can coexist in the same place!* These are two utterly different proclamations about the nature of the universe. In my experience, most Christians are very good theists who just happen to have named their god Jesus.

With dualistic minds it is always one or the other — it can never be both. The result is that we still think of ourselves as mere humans trying desperately to become "spiritual," when the Christian revelation was precisely that you are already spiritual ("in God"), and your difficult but necessary task is to learn how to become human. Jesus came to model the full integration for us (see 1 Corinthians 15:47–49) and, in effect, told us that Divinity looked just like him — while he looked ordinarily human to everybody!

It is in our humanity that we are still are so wounded, so needy, so unloving, so self-hating, and so in need of enlightenment. We seem to have spawned centuries of people trying to be spiritual and religious, whereas our record on basic humanness is rather pitiful.

Jesus himself seemed to caution his contemporaries to humility and patience before this subtle mystery of who he was: "You do not know where I came from and where I am going" (John 8:14); "No one knows the Father except the Son and those to whom the Son chooses to reveal him" (Matthew 11:27). He seemed to know that this mystery of being both divine and human would take a very long time to absorb, understand, accept, or reconcile. "Flesh and blood cannot do it," he tells Peter in Matthew 16:17. It is the ultimate paradox, and every Christian and every human being struggles with it anew, both in themselves and in him, and every day.

We could not hold the mystery together in Jesus, despite being assured that he is "the one single New Man" (Ephesians 2:15), the Archetypal Person who reconciles and recapitulates everything inside of himself (Colossians 1:15–20). The sad result is that we could not see, honor, and reconcile the mystery inside of ourselves or in one another. We could not let Jesus "save" us, you might say. *It is the third eye that allows us to say yes to the infinite mystery of Jesus and the infinite mystery that we are to ourselves. They are finally the same mystery.*

THE PRAYER OF JESUS

Jesus' own style of teaching in stories, parables, and enigmatic sayings was undoubtedly learned in his own prayer practices. He clearly operated from a consciousness different from that of the masses and even that of the religious leaders who largely fought him. Most seemed to misunderstand him, or even ignore him, despite what seem to be astounding healings and miracles. Yet he did not let that discourage him, and he merely ended his parabolic discourse by saying, "Happy are you that do see, and happy are you that do hear!" (Matthew 13:15). It is almost as if he recognized that contemplative/nondual seeing would be the exception and not the rule. How did he attain such freedom and authority? (Let's attempt to answer this without jumping too quickly to "because he was God!")

1. Jesus himself seemed to prefer a prayer of quiet, something more than social, liturgical, or verbal prayer, which is mentioned only a very few times. What we do hear are frequent references such as "In the morning, long before dawn, he got up and left the house and went off to a lonely place to pray" (Mark 1:35; also in Matthew 14:23 and Mark 1:12–13). Luke describes him as praying privately before almost all major events. There are the forty days alone in the desert, which means he must have missed the family-based Sabbath observances and the public temple services. And of course there is his final prayer alone in the Garden of Gethsemane.

2. His own teaching on prayer is profoundly instructive and direct:

   a. He warns his followers about the very real dangers of public prayer or "standing up in the synagogues" (Matthew 6:5), as he puts it. It does not seem that we have listened to that advice and insisted on a personal prayer journey to undergird and balance the explicit ego dangers of social prayer.

   b. "You should go to your private room, shut the door, and pray to your Father who is in that secret place" (Matthew 6:6). This is again rather explicit and also intimately invitational, especially because most homes of his people would have had no such thing as a private room.

   c. "In your prayers, do not babble on as the pagans do, thinking that by using many words they will make themselves be heard. Do not be like them!" (Matthew

6:7). Again, this is very direct, yet rather explicitly ignored by the traditions — Catholic, Orthodox, and Protestant — who often prefer public worship services and lots of words. (It keeps us clergy feeling useful.)

3. Luke, in his presentation of the only verbal prayer that Jesus ever taught, the Our Father (Lord's Prayer), offers a most telling introduction. He mentions that Jesus "was in a certain place praying," where he is interrupted by one of the disciples who has a request of him. "Lord, teach us to pray, just as John taught his disciples" (11:1–2). Groups were usually identified by having their official group prayer — something like the Serenity Prayer of Alcoholics Anonymous today. It identifies us and our spirituality to others and to ourselves. The very fact that they had to ask for it seems to imply that he had not given them a verbal prayer before! Perhaps it was even a concession.

When we emphasize public, verbal, and social prayer forms, along with group rituals, while not giving people any inner experience of their own inner aliveness (the "Indwelling Spirit"), it tends to keep religion on the level of a social contract; this is often what we call cultural Christianity or civil religion. We can perhaps see this more easily in Islam than we can see it in Christianity. Surely this is why the prophets so often criticized the priesthood, the sacrifices, and the sanctuary (Jeremiah 7:1–11, Isaiah 1:11–17, Amos 5:21–24, and Hosea 6:6, which was often quoted by Jesus).

Social and public prayers hold groups and religions together, but they do not necessarily transform people at any deep level. In fact, group certitude and solidarity often becomes a substitute for any real journey of our own. Hear this clearly. I am not saying there is no place for public prayer, but we do need to heed Jesus' very clear warnings about it. In my own church, I am afraid I have met many priests who have recited the Divine Office and performed Mass most days of their lives, yet who show little evidence of any inner life or depth. It is perhaps not a personal failure as much as a "structural sin." We all live inside of a common domain, which largely determines energy, depth, and how much we can hear or even imagine. As René Girard so well illustrated, we are imitative beings at the core. Our holiness is always the group's holiness first; our sin is invariably a social sin before it is our own.

Prayer conducted primarily in public becomes a matter of making announcements to God or to the group or to your own self-image. Jesus specifically says this is unnecessary since "your Father knows what you need before you ask him" (Matthew 6:9). Social prayer runs the risk of becoming an elevating of one's social image and one's self-image; this is exactly what Jesus points out and warns against in the story of the Publican and the Pharisee in Luke 18:9–14. Remember, the Pharisee says all the right things publicly and even does all the right things privately, but Jesus says he "went home not right with God." The other guy just beats his breast in the back of the synagogue, with no mention of any correct behavior at all, but "he went home right with God." Pretty amazing, considering what we emphasize in our religious teachings today!

What all of these teachings of Jesus seem to say is that we probably need "unsaying prayer," the prayer of quiet or contemplative prayer, to balance out and ground all "saying prayer." Many Christians seem to have little experience of prayer of quiet, and tend to actually be afraid of it or even condemn it. They have not been taught what to do with their overactive minds, and so they are afraid of silence. Without an inner life, our outer prayer will soon become superficial, ego-centered, and even counter-productive on the spiritual path. This is much of the import of all of Matthew 6, where Jesus emphasizes interiority and clari-fication of intention in each of the three spiritual disciplines — almsgiving, prayer, and fasting.

Western culture has tended to be an extroverted culture and a "can-do" culture. Prayer too easily became an attempt to change God and aggrandize ourselves instead of what it was meant to be — an interior practice *to change the one who is praying,* which will always happen if we stand calmly before this uncanny and utterly safe Presence, allowing the Divine Gaze to invade and heal our unconscious, the place where 95 percent of our motivations and reactions come from. *All we can really do is return the gaze.* Then, as Meister Eckhart so perfectly said, "the eye with which we look back at God will be the same eye that first looked at us." We just complete the circuit!

NOT HERE, NOT THERE

Ultimate Reality cannot be seen with any dual operation of the mind, where we eliminate the mysterious, the confusing — any-thing scary, unfamiliar, or outside our comfort zone. Dualistic thinking is not naked presence to the Presence, but highly con-trolled and limited seeing. With such software, we cannot access things like infinity, God, grace, mercy, or love — the necessary and important things! Wouldn't you join me in saying "I would not respect any God that I could figure out"? St. Augustine said the same in the fifth century: "**If you understand it, then it** *is not* **God**" (*Si comprehenderis, non est Deus*).

Such honoring and allowing of Mystery was consistently practiced by Jesus himself. So many of his sayings are so enigmatic and confusing that I am convinced that is why most Catholics simply stopped reading the Bible. If he had been primarily concerned about perfect clarity from his side, and obvious understanding on our side, he surely didn't do very well as a communicator, even in his lifetime. Protestants insisted on reading and studying the Scriptures, thank God, but then they were certain they had the one and only interpretation and ignored many of the others. This, even after Jesus so often (seven times in Matthew 13 alone) taught that the Ultimate Reality (which he calls "the kingdom") is always *like* something — clearly *a simile or metaphor, inviting further experience and journey*, not an idea with definitions that could be checked true or false on a student exam.

Jesus largely communicates through parables, stories, aphorisms, and often deeply obscure riddles (such as "Many are called, but few are chosen"). This is not discourse pleasing to systematic thinkers. If I had turned in papers as open to misunderstanding, false interpretation, and even heresy as most of Jesus' teachings are, I would never have passed any of my theology courses. He must have not been very concerned about exact words, or he would have learned to speak Greek, instead of the philosophically imprecise and very different Aramaic![21]

For our purposes here, I would like to point out one teaching in Luke's Gospel that I think is pivotal — one that, some would say, sounds almost exactly like the saying of a Zen Master. Jesus is addressing both the Pharisees and the disciples, therefore both outsiders and insiders at the same time.

In response to their question "*When* will the Kingdom come?" he tells them that Ultimate Reality is "not here and not there," taking us away from our typical attachment to time. "For the Ultimate Reality is 'within you'!" (Luke 17:21). If you let people concentrate too much on special times, feasts, services, and seasons, they forget it is always now and here when God happens. They stop living in the naked now and wait for Christmas or Easter, Sunday morning, or some far-off future day of enlightenment (see Colossians 2:16–19).

Then Jesus makes the identical point about place. When they ask, "*Where* should we look for the Day of the Coming?" he says, "Don't look here and don't look there" (Luke 17:23). Once you *over*-localize God's action in one place, church service, sacrament, or any other kind of event, we can easily conclude that it is *not* in another place — or even worse, that it is not available everywhere and all the time.

In relativizing both time and space, Jesus is doing something similar to what Eckhart Tolle is doing for many today with his "power of now." He makes us look for the Absolute in a different way than by "certain ideas." Any good spiritual teacher has to overcome both space and time, or they have no ability to give you a sense of the eternal and the Really Real. I would in fact say this is essential. Poor spiritual teaching is always saying "only" here and "only" there, such as "only in my church." Good spiritual teaching is saying "always" and "everywhere."[22]

Jesus concludes this dialogue with a most telling line. "You will long to see, but you will not see" (Luke 17:22). It is a judgment on all religion that is trapped in here *or* there, now *or* then. Even worse, in our spiritual blindness, we often applied such criticism of spiritual blindness to other people — such as "those incorrigible Jews" or "those Catholics" — thereby losing the essential point, which is the transformative message for ourselves. In both of these passages, Jesus is exactly repeating the Sanskrit *neti, neti* of ancient Hinduism. "Not this, not that" was taught by ancient sages to protect the final unpronounceability and full knowability of the Holy.

Jesus humbles much of organized religion's capacity to control the God-human relationship, because in effect, Jesus is saying that God is both now and always, here and there, and beyond any attempt to be controlled, to be bought and sold in any temple. He is protecting the utter freedom of God to be *where* God wants and *when* God wants and *who* God wants. Good theology always protects God's total freedom, and does not demand that God follow our rules. Jesus does this explicitly in John's Gospel several times: "The Spirit blows where it wills. You can hear and see it by its effects, but you do not know where it comes from or where it goes" (3:8). Also, "The hour is coming when you will worship the Father neither on this mountain nor in Jerusalem...but the hour will come when we will worship the Father in Spirit and truth" (4:21, 23).

How did we misinterpret such clear passages? For some reason, we forget that every time God forgives or shows mercy, God is breaking God's own rules, being inconsistent and rather nondualistic. Once you have known grace, your tit-for-tat universe is forever undone: God is everywhere and always and scandalously found even in the failure of sin. If God is truly victorious, how could it be otherwise?[23] In fact, there is no place left where God cannot be found. The Gospels never record Jesus having a single prerequisite for any of his healings: no affiliation with the right group, no moral worthiness, no attendance at the right temple, no purity codes, nothing except desire itself. Don't take my word for it: verify this for yourself.

Jesus is in effect saying that if God is everywhere, then God is not anywhere exclusively. We church employees tend not to like that. You can see why any attempt to organize the God experience moves toward an unconscious but nevertheless vested interest in keeping people in the dualistic mind, and therefore always a *little* insecure about grace and mercy and forgiveness. Groups hold together much better when there is a clear and defined "us" and "them" and when we are the superior ones.[24]

Conservatives tend to understand this much better than liberals do. Guilt-based religion, strong boundary markers, and shame work well to keep the troops in line. Of course, if, as the Scriptures state in so many different ways, there is "one God of all the earth," and if this God is "all-merciful," then this approach is finally unworkable. What is the cut-off point between worthiness and unworthiness? What is the cut-off point between those who are saved by mercy and those who are not? Who are the pure ones?

I remember being trained in the *Baltimore Catechism* as a little Catholic boy. One of the first questions (#16) was "Where is God?" The correct answer is "God is everywhere." And then the whole rest of the book proceeds to teach that such ubiquity is not really true! God was really only with Catholics, in our churches, in fact, really only in the tabernacle, and then only if the priest said a valid Mass, and then only available to "good" people who followed the rules. We have always been much better at "binding up" God than "loosening" divine availability, even though Jesus gave us *both* powers (Matthew 16:19). For some reason, we really do not want God to be everywhere, just here, and we of course end up losing God even for ourselves.

Poor God has always seemed to have a very hard time showing love or mercy to sinners, despite the fact that, according to Jesus, it is God's very job description (Romans 3:9ff). Instead of creating such obstacles, we have to start operating like the highway builder, valley filler, and mountain leveler that John the Baptist was (see Luke 3:5). When the temple priesthood started making God distant and elite, John just went down to the riverside and poured natural water over shamed bodies. That's why Jesus joined his offbeat ministry. His very initiation rite was a scathing critique of temple or official requirements, and how prone they are to missing the point.

Why did Jesus accept such an unofficial ritual? Was he trying to tell us something? What is it that Jesus, and all spiritual masters, is trying to achieve by this kind of useless, dangerous, and "fuzzy" thinking? Doesn't Jesus know that nothing lasts without organization and institution? Doesn't Jesus know that we need order, laws, and rules for society to hold together? Surely he does know all this, but he also knows that the only measure and criterion for spiritual things is God's infinite compassion (Luke 6:36; all of Luke 15) and never our ability to understand it or perfectly respond to it. He knows that *God does not love us because we are that good. God loves us because God is good.* That changes everything.

THE TWO HEELS OF A CHRISTIAN ACHILLES

Here is the problem. We impose our either-or mentality onto God and largely make much of Jesus' central teaching on grace and mercy an impossible concept to process. It gets worse. We also apply all-or-nothing thinking to ourselves, making the message impossible to obey on any honest level. As a result, we are forced to pretend, repress, deny, or become a hypocrite, because nothing human is or ever will be perfect enough, worthy enough, or pure enough. It is not so much that hypocrites join religious groups, but that the very structures of much religion encourage people to act and pretend. This all-or-nothing thinking is a cancer at the heart of our preached message, and it takes two major forms:

1. The individual Christian is told to love unconditionally, but the God who commands this is depicted as having a very conditional and quite exclusive love himself or herself! The believer is told to love his enemies, but "God" clearly does not; in fact, God punishes them for all eternity. This stifles and paralyzes many believers at the conscious or unconscious level, and it should. Such a message will not save the world and surely will not produce many great or loving people. The many loving Christians I have met in my life usually have had at least one unconditionally loving parent or friend along the way, and God was then able to second the motion. There are remarkable exceptions to this, however. I have met a few humanly unloved people whose need for divine love was so great that they surrendered to it — utterly. The Gospel worked for them.

2. Under the message that most of us have heard, we end up being more loving than God, and then not taking God very seriously. Even my less-than-saintly friends, the ordinary Joes on the block, would usually give a guy a break, overlook some mistakes, and even on their worst days would not imagine torturing people who do not like them, worship them, or believe in them. "God" ends up looking rather petty, needy, narcissistic, and easily offended. God's offended justice is clearly much stronger than God's mercy, it seems. Why would anyone trust or love such a God, or want to be alone with Him or Her? Much less spend eternity with such a Being? I wouldn't. We must come to recognize that this perspective, conscious or unconscious, is at the basis of much agnosticism and atheism in the West today.

My intention is not to be unfair or negative in stating this so straightforwardly, but we must start being honest about the way what we call "good news" has ended up being bad news for many sincere human beings who really want to believe. Often, these are people of real inner integrity or spiritual intelligence, who refuse to deny, repress, or pretend. I have met them too often, and they usually feel lost, angry, and abandoned, like an abused child would feel.

Jesus comes at these questions from exactly the opposite side and arrives at a much better conclusion: "If you who are evil, know how to give your children what is good, then how much more God?" (Matthew 7:11). He takes God out of the straightjacket we have imposed on God, and lets God's unconditional love set the only standard and measuring stick. Then Christian spirituality becomes very simply the *imitatio Dei,* the imitation of God (Ephesians 5:1): to love one another and ourselves *exactly the way God loves us.*

As history has shown, if you don't get the first premise right — God's love is absolutely unconditional — the whole thing falls apart. You cannot arrive at an unconditionally loving God or an unconditionally loving self with the dualistic mind, because there will always be contrary evidence that puts you back into some kind of worthiness contest. Such people are also invariably drawn to the regressive dualistic texts in the Scriptures, which only reinforce their own violence and their fears.[25]

After almost forty years of teaching and preaching, I can say: You see the text through your available eyes. You hear a text from your own level of development and consciousness.[26] Punitive people love punitive texts; loving people hear in the same text calls to discernment, clarity, choice, and decision. "And between the two there is a great gulf, not allowing one to cross from one side to another" (Luke 16:26). All we can do is help people grow up, and then they hear Scripture maturely. Dualistic, early-stage thinking will murder the most merciful of texts, because that is where they are. *We do not see things as they are; we see things as we are.* Take that as nearly certain.

God, however, swims in an ocean of mercy, with plenty of room for the outsider, the sinner, and even the violent, according to the Scriptures. The crucified Jesus calls for no recrimination against his killers, and he reminds us, "I did not come to make the virtuous feel good about themselves, but for those who need a doctor" (Mark 2:17). The Great Forgiver calls us all inside of God's universal breath (John 20:22). Or as the poet puts it,

> Wild air, world-mothering air,
> Nestling me everywhere, . . .
> I say that we are wound
> With mercy round and round,
> As if with air, the same . . .
> And makes, O marvelous!
> New Nazareths in us.
> — Gerard Manley Hopkins,
> "Compared to the Air
> We Breathe"

In the world of religion, nondual seers are the only experts. Sinners, saints, lovers, and poets, and all those who have swum in this ocean of mercy can hold contrary evidence together because they have allowed God to first of all do it in them — over and over again. They have inhaled the Great Air, the One Breath, the Holy Spirit that first gave Adam life and winds us all "round and round."

To these ever new Adams and ever new Eves, Jesus the human always makes sense — supreme sense, common sense, spiritual sense, joyful sense. Head and heart and body finally work together as one, and we are back in the garden with him, naked and unashamed.

CHAPTER ELEVEN

Conversion

Begin by Changing the Seer

And the Word became flesh.
—JOHN 1:14

Mere words have something of quicksand about them. Only
experience is the rope that is thrown to us.
— GEORGES BATAILLE

Conversion is a crucial idea for understanding how the mystics
see. Yet conversion is not the exclusive domain of hermits and
ecstatics; even brilliant academic theologians have recognized its
importance. Among the great thinkers who, like so many Jesuits,
have inspired me and helped me integrate my study and experience with church politics and practice is Bernard Lonergan
(1904–84), and particularly his brilliant theories of knowledge
and "insight." He observed that after the scientific (practical and
empirical) mind gained prominence, it became difficult not to
think of God as merely the result of pie-in-the-sky conditioning,
because clearly this God could not be verified in any laboratory
or with our newly discovered methods.

HEALING THE OBSERVER

In the face of these great challenges, Lonergan suggested that
we needed a new "foundation for knowledge" because the old

foundations would no longer do. He was fascinated by the scientific mind and method, and rightly felt it had much to offer religion, but he also felt that religion had much to offer science, especially in regard to method and the cleansing of the seer.

While never denying the objectivity of truth, Lonergan claimed that most religious people have "an exaggerated view of the objectivity of truth" and especially their capacity to understand it.[27] It is a humorous paradox that in a faith that speaks about the "journey" of following Jesus, Christians claim to have total and absolute truth from the beginning, while scientists, who are supposedly largely atheists and agnostics, are quite willing to work for decades knowing that their theories and hypotheses are merely provisional.[28]

Lonergan taught that the only real way to find objectivity today was to help people clarify and heal their subjectivity! These words might remind us of the Buddha. But Lonergan gave a very old-fashioned Christian word for that process — "conversion." He believed and tried to demonstrate that the process of conversion was itself the great clarifier and was the healing of our own woundedness, neediness, and egocentricity so that true seeing could be possible, insofar as it is possible. He sounded a bit like William Blake: "All we need to do is cleanse the doors of perception, and we shall see things as they are — infinite."

Authentically converted people would see truth, as far as humans are able and would see it in a way that could be shared, at least with other converted people. I know how "safe" and energized I feel when I am sharing even my most offbeat ideas with truly holy or loving people — or good therapists. Perhaps you know this feeling as well. You know they will understand what you are searching to say. Among antagonistic, insecure, or dualistic people, you always feel unsafe. Lonergan moved from searching for and arguing about airy abstractions to changing the seer himself or herself. This was his "new foundation" for truth-seeking. This was a remarkable breakthrough for the West, in my opinion, and in part he learned it from scientists, who knew the connection between the seer and the seen.

Jesus, not accidentally, sent his apostles to "fish for people." We have spent much of our history instead clarifying and defending concepts and organizations — fishing much more for right ideas than people. Lonergan boldly says that "conversion is the experience by which one becomes an authentic human being." My assumption would be that human beings attract other human beings to the same level of awareness — just by being, as St. Irenaeus put it, "fully alive." This inherent attraction, and not the self-promotion of my ideas versus your ideas, is how we must "fish" inside of religion.

This same idea is found in the Twelve Traditions of Bill Wilson and others — that Alcoholics Anonymous will advance *much more by attraction than by promotion,* more by competence in actually doing the job than by praising itself for promising to do the job. The church might have something to learn from alcoholics!

It comes down to this: transformed people transform people.

THREE LEVELS OF CONVERSION

For Lonergan, full Christian conversion has three important levels.

1. **Intellectual conversion**: "Moving out of a world of mere sense perception and arriving, dazed and disoriented for a while, into a universe of being."[29] This sounds like what we are calling third-eye seeing, seeing as the mystics see.

2. **Moral conversion**: Despite the word "moral," this kind of conversion is not what you might think: giving up your drink, your money, and your sexual thoughts. It is more subtle — a purification of your real motives for doing things (even good things) from the usual desires for personal satisfaction, a need for control personally or socially, or any craving to build up the ego or feel good about yourself. Instead, you shift to the honest perception of value outside of yourself. I am convinced that Lonergan is right: When people can seek the true good and the common good, even when it is of no ego advantage to them, you have a morally converted person.[30]

3. **Religious conversion**: Religious conversion occurs when we allow ourselves to live as a *Being-in-Love* who is "held, grasped, possessed, and owned through a total and so otherworldly love."[31] Only then are we spiritually converted. Transformation into love is the heart of religious conversion, for Lonergan and all the saints, because, of course, God is love. This is not at all the same as simply joining a church, believing things to be true or false, or having a strong opinion on such topics as abortion, gay marriage, or health care reform.

Mind you, it takes Lonergan several books to make these subtle points, and I am greatly simplifying him, but just enough so that many of us ordinary Franciscan types can grasp the momentous change here. "The new foundation," for Lonergan, "consists not in objective statements but in subjective reality."[32] That is the basis for his objectivity — transformed people who see what is really there. It is the same movement Jesus is making when he makes truth into a person instead of an abstract concept: "I am the way, the truth, and the life" (John 14:6). Authentic people like Jesus both see and are truth. Because they are "true," they can see truth.

Lonergan is correct. This is not to say there is no place for rational thinking, which he would call being "attentive, intelligent, and reasonable" — but this is not easily achieved, and *never without authentic conversion first.* Mature religion involves changing ourselves and letting ourselves be changed by a mysterious encounter with grace, mercy, and forgiveness. This is the truth that will set us free (John 8:32). Yet much of our history has involved trying to change *other* people — with *our* ideas. This has gotten us almost nowhere, and it allows us to remain untransformed and unconverted ourselves.

> **Remember, it is only transformed people who have the power to transform others, as if by osmosis. Usually you can lead others only as far as you yourself have gone. Too often we try to push, intimidate, threaten, cajole, and manipulate others. It seldom works, because *that is not the way the soul works.* In the presence of whole people, or any encounter with Holiness Itself, we simply find that, after a while, we are different — and much better! Then we wonder how we got there. If we are spiritually smart, we will look for Someone Else to thank.**

CHAPTER TWELVE

Change Your Mind

*Ultimate Reality is at hand! Change your mind and believe
such good news!* — MARK 1:15

We have all seen cartoons of an angry, bearded man walking
around holding or wearing the sign "Repent!" If the sign is large
enough, he might even carry the entire Bible verse: "Repent, for
the kingdom of God is at hand!" The message is seemingly that
you'd better get ready for the judgment of an angry God who
will punish you for your sins. The presumed solution is to join
a church, believe the right set of religious ideas, or get rid of
your gin.

But did anyone ever tell you that Jesus' very first message in
the Gospels, which is usually translated as "convert," "repent,"
or "reform" (Matthew 4:17, Mark 1:15) is the Greek word
metanoia, which quite literally means to "change your mind"?
Jesus first word to us was "change!" — and *mind* change at that!
What we have translated as "repent" is not a moralistic or even
churchy word at all; it is a clear strategy for enlightenment for the
world. Once you accept ongoing change as a central program for
yourself, you tend to continue growing throughout all of your life.

Jesus knows that self-critical, yet not negative, people will
always keep growing and engaging with the world around them,
with themselves, and with God. They will especially flourish
inside of difficulties. The rest of us use our minds to close down,

89

close off, and avoid all change. The ego and the false self hate change more than anything else in the world, and the mind is their primary control tower.

In clear and unmistakable language, the Hebrew prophets, Mohammed, and Jesus were talking about people changing. Yet how is it that the groups that formed in their names frequently became bulwarks against change? So often, we have been protectors of the past, lovers of empire, power, and business as usual — especially when the present arrangement was to our advantage. In fact, if you ask most people how they view religion, they'll answer that it is supposed to be a protector of the tradition. This is why, for so much of our history, we have made good bedfellows with kings, queens, dictators, and repressive regimes. Just ask the French, the English, the Spanish, the Germans, the Austrians, the Russians, almost all Latin Americans, and Protestant North Americans. We have consistently been on the side of our particular *ancien régime* instead of the transnational kingdom of God, ever since Constantine invited us into his palaces in A.D. 313.

THE EGO HATES CHANGE

Why so much status quo? Once you know that the one thing the ego hates more than anything else is *change,* it makes perfect sense why most people hunker down into mere survival. Whether because of abuse and oppression or other causes, defended and defensive selves will do anything rather than change — even acting against their own best interest. Ask any addict or member of a tightly defined group. Ego is just another word for blindness. The ego self is by my definition *the unobserved self,* because once you see it, the game is over.[33]

The ego must remain unseen and disguised to be effective in protecting itself. Evil always depends on denial and disguise, it seems (2 Corinthians 11:14). The ego as such is not evil, but it can lead us to do evil without realizing it. (Paul's word for ego was "flesh.") To succeed, evil somehow has to look like virtue. It leaves you blind to your own illusions and convinced that you see perfectly. This is at the heart of the problem of conversion and the very nature of spiritual transformation.

Most people have not been offered a different mind, only different behaviors, beliefs, and belonging systems. They do not necessarily nourish us, much less transform us. But they invariably secure us and validate us where we already are. They are what I and others have called "the task of the first half of life."[34] Required behaviors and beliefs are good and necessary to get us started. But when we invest in them too heavily, they soon become places to hide. As Paul says, they are just a "nursemaid" to get us started (Galatians 3:24), or as I like to call them, training wheels. If we hold on to them too tightly and for too long, we never internalize values and strengths — we never "grow up." Isn't this true of a lot of people you know? Is it true of you, too?

DIFFERENT RELIGIONS, SAME EGO RESISTANCE

This ego resistance leaves many folks with the peculiar attitude that might be stated in this way: "One of us is wrong, and it is surely not me." Fundamentalist Christians can recognize this pattern in Muslims but not in themselves. Warlike Jews can recognize it in Christians but not in themselves. Radical Muslims can recognize aggressiveness in Jews but not in themselves. Religion should have done much better in enlightening its own.

The terms "liberal" and "conservative" invariably refer to rather useless polarity thinking, and thus they are not a very helpful distinction and lens for truth. But if you know only dualistic thinking, you are trapped inside that small frame. Unself-critical liberals are just as problematic as unself-critical conservatives. Liberals protect themselves by dualistic *suspicion* judgments, making them overly dismissive of those they consider authorities or the top. Conservatives protect themselves by dualistic *worthiness* judgments, making them overly dismissive of what they judge to be the bottom. Both engage in their own kind of superiority system. Unself-critical Christians are no more the hope of the world than are unself-critical Muslims or Jews. There is often not much difference between different religions and political parties at the ego level — only the vocabulary, rituals, and conversation circles differ. "We all go where we get our backs scratched."

Although successful corporations thrive on outside consultants, feedback, suggestions, and brainstorming, by changing constantly and rewarding self-criticism, in religious circles it is considered a sign of disobedience, rebellion, heresy, or even disbelief to question, think about, or change ideas or authorities. Words are to be repeated and memorized, rituals are not to be changed, and behaviors are judged externally and almost mechanically.

Apparently, that is why most of the prophets, including Jesus himself, were killed *by their own.* When you show a capacity for positive criticism and "incorporate the negative," you inevitably draw forth serious opposition from those of your own group. "You are not loyal, faithful, or patriotic," the uncritical insider says. Thus the "prophet," a professional inside critic, was a protected office in Israel and even in the early church. Paul lists it as the second most important gift for the church, after apostles (1 Corinthians 12:28), yet in recent centuries it has largely disappeared. How is it that today the institutions that claim to be scriptural have forgotten that necessary role and task? Again, these are not bad people, but simply other examples of what dualistic thinking *cannot* achieve.

Our bearded man inside the sandwich board, with REPENT written on each side for others to see, needs to turn the sign around and recognize that it is first of all telling *him* to change! If he would, he might stop accusing or intimidating others, and we might have true "repentance." The Satanic impulse is always accusing others, but never himself or herself, as the very word reveals (*Satan* = the Accuser).

INERTIA RESISTS CHANGE

The Law of Inertia: the tendency of a body to resist change of course or acceleration

We create much of our own opposition when we refuse to change. This happened to the United States after September 11, 2001. On September 12 we had people around the world on our side, but paranoid, oppositional thinking set in at almost all levels. (We can't blame just the president!) A year later, much of the world mistrusted or even hated America. If there had been even slight self-criticism, or freedom to publicly ask the question "Why does so much of the world hate us?" or "How could America change?" we might have diffused the rage of thousands of angry young men all over the earth. They will now be around for a long time and will pass on their hatred to the next generation. We actually operated against our own self-interest, but the mind not open to change cannot see that. It is too trapped inside of polarity thinking. It is so eager to shoot at something that it shoots itself in the foot and does not even realize it.

Within the Christian churches, how else can we explain the obvious avoidance of so many of Jesus' major teachings? Jesus' direct and clear teachings on issues such as nonviolence, a simple lifestyle, love of the poor, forgiveness, love of enemies, inclusivity, mercy, and not seeking status, power, perks, and possessions: throughout history, all have been overwhelmingly ignored by mainline Christian churches, even those who call themselves orthodox or biblical.

This avoidance defies explanation until we understand how dualistic thinking protects and pads the ego and its fear of change. Notice that the things we ignored above require *actual change* of our lifestyle, our security systems, or our dualistic thought patterns. The things we emphasized instead were usually intellectual beliefs or moral superiority stances that asked little of us: the divinity of Christ, the virgin birth, the atonement theory, and beliefs about reproduction and sex. After a while, you start recognizing the underlying bias. The ego diverts your attention from anything that would ask *you* to change, to righteous causes that invariably ask *others* to change.

How did we end up with this 180-degree change in message and not even see it? This is the spiritual form of the law of inertia. Humans prefer what we are accustomed to; we want to go with the prevailing flow, the conveyer belt. Society and church needed and wanted security systems, status symbols, wealth, and warfare. We could not see them as sin corporately, so we did not see them as sin individually, either. Social need and cultural inertia primarily determine much of people's morality. It took till John Paul II for a pope to finally speak of "social sin" and "structural evil." Until then, we largely praised or shamed individuals, while letting nation states run morally unchecked. We were led to dismiss all countercultural wisdom as poetry, idealism — seen as not practical in the real world, if not just impossible.[35]

Were the people influenced in this way stupid and selfish? Some were, of course, but many were not. They might have done better if they had been offered religion as ego transformation ("unless the grain of wheat dies") instead of religion as group superiority, or religion as God's demand for us to have correct ideas about things, or religion as a moral worthiness contest to win entrance into the next world.[36]

HEAVEN AND HELL:
YOU MUST CHANGE AGAIN AND AGAIN

Even heaven and hell, pedagogical images that appear in various forms in most religions, became primarily geographical places of reward and punishment that kept us from seeing what was first of all within us, around us, and right now. Pope John Paul II himself said that heaven and hell were primarily "states of consciousness."[37] Simone Weil, however, named it the best. She said, "Inner communion is good for the good and bad for the bad. God invites all the damned into paradise, but for them it is hell."

Heaven is *now and forever* for those who are willing to keep changing, even for "the bad" whom God forever entices into a state of communion, a letting go into love. As soon as we change into communion we are immediately in heaven. So we all had better become well-practiced at changing! As St. Catherine of Siena put it, "It is heaven all the way to heaven, and it is hell all the way to hell." The logically necessary concept of hell is an urgent warning against the fatal and eternal consequences of not changing into communion. It indeed kills the soul.

If your religious practice is nothing more than to remain sincerely open to the ongoing challenges of life and love, you *will* find God — and also yourself. Keeping the heart spaces and the mind spaces open, sometimes even "in hell," is the essential work of spirituality. The great Cardinal Newman said that "to be human is to change, to be perfect is to have changed many times." Great people keep adjusting to what life offers them and what life demands of them. Even the intelligence of animals is measured by their ability to cleverly adjust to new circumstances. Why should we be any different?

You might think that change means losing your sense of order or risking making a mistake, including a mistake about your belief in God. Yet even that's okay, because the deadening alternative is much worse. The Holy One does not really need your loyal verbal protection. God's love is so ingenious and victorious that I find God is willing to turn the world around to get me facing in the right direction. God seems to be *totally* into change. I know this every time I see how divine grace maneuvers around my sinfulness and human events, and how the entire universe itself is continually changing states from solids to liquids to gasses to seeming emptiness. Change is God's clear pattern. Surely, we are not greater than God.

If certitude, predictability, and perfect order were so important, Jesus would have come in a time of digital recorders and cameras, and he would have at least written his ideas down somewhere — and more clearly! He would have described his task as the establishing of archives instead of a sprawling banquet of rich food and wine, as he consistently did. He said, "I have come that you might have life, and a very abundant life at that" (John 10:10). How did we ever get correct rational ideas confused with an abundant life? This happens perhaps to folks who are unwilling to let go of their attachment to their images of themselves, the world, and God. They will not let go of their attachments for a living relationship. "The old wine is good enough," they say (Luke 5:39), and so they miss out on the great banquet that all the mystics, the prophets, and Jesus describe. (See Isaiah 25:6-7, 55:1-2, John 2:1-12, and most of Luke 14.)

Surely God does not exist so that we can think correctly about Him — or Her. Amazingly and wonderfully, like all good parents, God desires instead the flourishing of what God created and what God loves — us ourselves. Ironically, we flourish more by *learning* from our mistakes and changing than by a straight course that teaches us nothing.

CHAPTER THIRTEEN

Things "Too Good to Be True"

From Polarity Thinking to Prayer

We must teach not in the way philosophy is taught, but in the way that the Spirit teaches. We must teach spiritual things spiritually. — 1 CORINTHIANS 2:13

The Spirit comes to help us in our weakness. When we cannot choose words in order to pray properly, the Spirit herself expresses that plea in a way that could never be put into words. — ROMANS 8:26

The idea of the third eye can seem foreign to both our culture and our experience, but in fact, you are experiencing an image of the third eye at this very moment. Take a look around you. Even though your own two eyes clearly look at all things from two distinct angles, they connect in the one brain and create one image that you take for granted as full and true perception. Yet why do you then say that *your* seeing is perfectly correct? Your own brain has offered you an example of two different angles and the reconciliation of difference. Your brain has already created a third eye that sees something different than either of the two on their own. This fact of physiology offers us a powerful metaphor for what we are talking about.

Ancient Hinduism actually painted a third eye onto the forehead. The *tika,* which originally was a sign of this new seeing or enlightenment, eventually became a cosmetic decoration for women, as it is today. This is similar to the crosses many Christians now wear as jewelry. Perhaps both are metaphors for what has happened to religion in our day.

REFRAMING FALSE DILEMMAS

As we said before, the human mind prefers to think by comparison and differentiation-from. It starts as a binary system, something like a computer. Polarity thinking is unfortunately a self-canceling system, a form of argumentation that merely lets both sides more deeply invest in and identify with their position. Words can always be fashioned to make our point, and even *we* know that it is not necessarily objectively or totally true. Ask any lawyer or judge, or honest husband and wife, if that is not the case. If truth is so obvious, why would we need a Supreme Court to resolve disputes? And even the justices disagree with one another, often vociferously!

Thus most groups divide into liberals and conservatives of some sort, thinking that by defeating the other, they will win. This appeals to our competitive nature. The truth, however, is always something other than what one side says about the other.

The creating of false alternatives to force a person into an either-or choice, which can occur even with well-intentioned people, is even more characteristic of hostile or insincere opponents, as we see the enemies of Jesus exemplify. "Is it permissible to pay taxes to Caesar or not?" they ask (Luke 20:22). Polarity thinking avoids all subtlety and discrimination and creates false dichotomies. If you fight dualistic thinkers directly, you are forced to become dualistic yourself. This is why, classically, Jesus sidesteps the two alternatives by telling a story, keeping silent, or sometimes presenting a third alternative that utterly reframes the false dilemma. Rhetorically, Jesus was really a genius.

Early in their struggles, all nonviolent teachers learn some form of this wisdom, which is also the wisdom of Solomon (recall his brilliant reframing in 1 Kings 3:16–28). If they didn't, they could not be nonviolent, as we see in Gandhi, Martin Luther King, Dorothy Day, and Mother Teresa. For example, I was told personally by the leadership sisters in Calcutta that Mother Teresa never tried to convert a Muslim or a Hindu to Catholicism. She told the sisters that their job was not to talk about Jesus or even promote Jesus, but *to be Jesus!* Is that radical "identity transplant" what we are avoiding? Or does dualistic thinking just deem it impossible?

ALTERNATIVE CONSCIOUSNESS

Religion at the more mature levels invariably learned an alternative consciousness, which was necessary for wider seeing and for addressing the great dilemmas of life. Some call it by the various names of light, including *enlightenment* (Hinduism, Buddhism, John's Gospel), some call it *conversion* (the falling of scales from Paul's eyes in Acts 9:18–19), Jesus calls several people who see correctly and act on it quite simply *saved* (see Luke 8:48, 17:19, Mark 7:28); or, in words almost too simple, "Do this and *life* is yours" (Luke 10:28). I agree with Jim Marion that Jesus' primary metaphor for this new consciousness was "the kingdom of God."[38] He is not talking about a place, or an afterlife, but a way of seeing and thinking now. The kingdom of God is the naked now — the world without human kingdoms, ethnic communities, national boundaries, or social identifications. That is about as subversive and universalist as you can get. But don't think about that too much; it will surely change your politics and your pocketbook.

How different this is from our later notion of salvation, which pushed the entire issue into the future and largely became a reward and punishment system. How different from Jesus' "the kingdom of heaven is in your midst" (Luke 17:21) or Paul's "Now is the day of salvation" (2 Corinthians 6:2). Healthy religion is always about seeing and knowing something *now*, which demands a transformation of consciousness on my part today, not moral gymnastics or heroic will power to earn a prize later.

PRAYER IS RESONANCE

The traditional and most universal word to describe a different access to truth was simply "to pray about something." But that lovely word "prayer" has been so deadened by pious use and misuse that we now have to describe this different mental attitude with new words. I am going to introduce a different word here, so you can perceive prayer in a fresh way, and perhaps appreciate what we mean by contemplation. The word is "resonance." Prayer is actually setting out a tuning fork. All you can really do in the spiritual life is get tuned to receive the always present message. Once you are tuned, you *will* receive, and it has nothing to do with worthiness or the group you belong to, but only inner resonance and a capacity for mutuality (Matthew 7:7–11). The

Sender is absolutely and always present and broadcasting; the only change is with the receiver station.

Prayer is indeed the way to make contact with God/Ultimate Reality, but it is not an attempt to change God's mind about us or about events. Such attempts are what the secularists make fun of — and rightly so. It is primarily about changing *our mind* so that things like infinity, mystery, and forgiveness can resound within us. The small mind cannot see Great Things because the two are on two different frequencies or channels, as it were. The Big Mind can know big things, but we must change channels. Like will know like.

Without prayer, the best you can do is know by comparison, calculation, and from the limited viewpoint of "you."[39] Prayer, as very traditionally understood, knows reality in a totally different way. Instead of presenting a guarded self to the moment, true prayer stops defending or promoting its ideas and feelings, lets go of any antagonistic attitudes or fears, and waits for, expects, and receives guidance from Another. It offers itself "nakedly" to the now, so that *your inner and aroused lover can meet the Lover*. Now you surely see why you have to allow some major surgery in your own heart, mind, and eyes to even pray at all (see Matthew 5:23–26). *Prayer is about changing you, not about changing God.*

Most simply put, as we've seen, prayer is something that happens *to you* (Romans 8:26–27), much more than anything *you privately do*. It is an allowing of the Big Self more than an assertion of the small self. Eventually you will find yourself preferring to say, "Prayer happened, and *I* was there" more than "I prayed today." All you know is that you are being led, being guided, being loved, being used, being prayed through — and you are no longer in the driver's seat. God stops being an object of attention like any other object in the world, and becomes at some level your own "I am." You start knowing through, with, and in Somebody Else. Your little "I Am" becomes "We Are." Please trust me on this. It might be the most important thing I am saying in this book.

EXPERIENCE IMPOSSIBLE AND IMPROBABLE THINGS

This experience is nothing I can prove to you. If I could prove it, it would not be nondual. But you will know it for yourself *when you let it happen* — but as I will continue to say, only after the fact. After you have allowed such a realization, and a very different quality of thought, you will know for yourself. It is available to everybody for the taking. Afterward you know instinctively that *your life is not about you, but you are about Life.*[40] "I live now not I, but I live another life," as Paul so poetically puts it in Galatians 2:20.

This is undoubtedly why Jesus warns us in several settings, "Don't talk about these things, until after [your humanity] is raised from the dead" (Matthew 17:9). To move from polarity thinking to prayer thinking is like being raised from the dead. You only know you have been raised after you are on the other side of the divide, but it is almost impossible to convince anyone who has not yet allowed that passover. They think you are talking silly or poetically, or they think you are claiming to be better or holier than they are. This has nothing at all to do with it. You have just passed over to the other side of awareness — and you know it was done to you! You are like the prophet Habakkuk, picked up by the hair and set elsewhere (Daniel 14:36).

There are so many wonderful things that polarity thinking will not allow you to know, whereas prayer thinking will allow you to trust and even experience improbable things, things too good to be true. So many Scriptures will now jump off the page at you. Things like this: "My dear people, we are *already* the children of God, and all we know is that *when the future is revealed we shall be just like him*" (1 John 3:2).

You are already a child of God, equipped with everything you need to begin resonating with the divine. That does not mean you are morally or psychologically perfect. Not at all. But *you will now have the freedom to see such failings in yourself, to grow and to love better because of them*. That is the major and important difference! "But if this is true," you may wonder, "how could I have gone through life without anyone teaching me this? How is such a great truth unknown to or forgotten by so much of the world, and even by the church?" To understand this, we turn our attention now to the lost tradition.

CHAPTER FOURTEEN

The Lost Tradition

All creation is groaning in one great act of giving birth.
— ROMANS 8:22

I still have many things to say to you, but they would be too much for you now. — JOHN 16:12

You can see that in this book I am a man of one major idea: immediate, unmediated contact with the moment is the clearest path to divine union; naked, undefended, and nondual presence has the best chance of encountering the Real Presence. I am approaching this theme in a hundred ways, because I know most of us have one hundred levels of resistance, denial, or avoidance, and for some reason, in our complicated world, *it is very hard to teach very simple things.* Any "mystery," by definition, is pregnant with hundreds of levels of unfolding and realization. That is especially true of the "tree of life" that is contemplative awareness.

I call contemplation the tree of life, as compared to the other tree "in the center of the garden" of Eden, "the tree of the knowledge of good and evil" (Genesis 2:9), because these two serve as ideal metaphors for the two minds. The tree of the knowledge of good and evil represents "either-or" dualism, which we are strictly warned against, and even told not to eat. The tree of life promises access to eternal things (3:22), grows "crops twelve times a year," and sprouts "leaves that are for the healing of the nations" (Revelation 22:2). It accesses the deep ground of God and of the self. The contemplative, nondual mind is a tree of continual and constant fruitfulness for the soul and for the world.

A binary system of either/or choices is good and necessary in the lofty worlds of logic, mechanics, mathematics, and science, and in the everyday world of knowing whether to turn left or right to get from point A to point B. It produced the scientific and industrial revolutions that have served us so well in many areas. But these have begun to show their severe limitations, and this mind can take us only so far; it cannot access eternal things. It is not the tree of life, but only the tree of "this or that."

Any allowing of the hidden side of things, the "more" side of things, the dark side of things — while also holding onto the attractive and knowable side — usually marks the beginnings of nondual consciousness. Whenever we can appreciate the goodness and value of something, while still knowing its limitations and failures, this also marks the beginnings of wisdom and nondual consciousness.

Most humans are not very good at such "allowing"; it often feels like what Paul calls "groaning." In recent centuries no one has shown us exactly how to do this, yet it is surely the tree of life at the center of the garden, whose roots extend deep and wide. Perhaps a more familiar word is simply "forgiveness." The struggle to forgive reality for being exactly what it is right now often breaks us through to nondual consciousness. We have to overcome the rational domination of ego and reason to forgive a deep hurt or memory. As Zechariah says in his beautiful canticle, "You will know salvation through the mystery of forgiveness" (Luke 2:77). That's it!

You cannot bypass the necessary tension of holding contraries and inconsistencies together, if you are to live on this earth.

These earthly experiences, these daily presentations will teach you nonduality in a way that is no longer theoretical or abstract. It becomes obvious in everything and everybody, every idea and every event, almost hidden in plain sight. Everything created is mortal and limited and, if you look long enough, always paradoxical.[41] By paradox, I mean something that initially looks contradictory or impossible, but in a different frame or at a different level is in fact deeply true.

I want to emphasize that it is a holding of a real tension, and not necessarily a balancing act, a closure, or any full resolution. It is agreeing to live without resolution, at least for a while. This is very different, and difficult for most people, largely because we have not been taught how to do this mentally or emotionally. We didn't know we could — or even should. We cannot see what we are never told to look for; we cannot do what is never offered as do-able. As Paul seems to say (and I partially paraphrase), hope would not be the virtue that it is if it led us to quick closure and we did not have to "wait for it with patience" (Romans 8:24–25). Simone Weil, the renowned Jewish-Christian seeker, felt this was the very nature of faith and spiritual searching. She had an extraordinary ability to hold creative tensions in ways that seem impossible — "larger than life" — to most of us.

I think this "opening and holding pattern" is the very name and description of *faith.* But faith in Christianity largely became believing things to be true or false (faith as intellectual assent) instead of giving people concrete practices so they could themselves know how to open up (faith), hold on (hope), and allow an infilling from another source (love). There are some practices offered throughout this book and in the appendices so that these virtues can be "practiced." But God gives us real practices every day of our lives, such as irritable people, long stop lights, and our own inconsistencies.

We must move from a belief-based religion to a practice-based religion, or little will change. We will merely continue to argue about what we are supposed to believe and who the unbelievers are. Consider the wisdom taught in the ancient aphorisms and stories of Hinduism, Confucianism, Taoism, Sufism, Zen, Buddhism, the Jewish prophets, and Jesus. There is a reason that so much of even Jesus' teaching feels abstruse, naïve, or irrelevant to us today. We no longer have the code for deciphering his parables today, with only rational, dualistic thought available to most of us. For example, the man coming at the last hour receives the same reward as the one who worked all day. This makes no sense at all to a dualistic mind or to anyone who rushes toward a quick judgment. So we reject the story or merely forget that he said it.

For the West, Jesus represents the new mind most strongly, and almost singularly, but it was only carried through by the Desert Fathers and Mothers of the first centuries, held on to inside of early monasticism, especially in Hesychastic and Celtic Christianity, and since then by a clear line of saints, monks, mystics, and recluses, who invariably had to separate in some way from the mainstream to preserve their sanity. In many cases we called it "religious life" and thereby accepted a two-tiered system that allowed mainline institutions to resist nondual thought.

THE DECLINE OF CONTEMPLATION

In time, at least in the Catholic world, many monks, nuns, and friars became workers for the institution, accepted its protocols, and often lost our own deeper traditions of transformation —

what we called our charisms. We morphed into "Churchianity" more than any genuine, transformative Christianity. While the two need not be in opposition, we were schooled in systematic theology, running schools to create more Catholics, and the administration of sacraments more than the Gospel lifestyle itself. And it is primarily a lifestyle!

Today, many Christians do not even know what we mean by the "Gospel life" because it became a belief and belonging system more than a full lifestyle. This much-needed synthesis of institution and inner experience or charism is what my own father, St. Francis, and many others along the way have always been trying to recover. It is seldom a full balance, but usually a holding of a creative tension, with much discouragement in between. But the balancing act is itself the very way we go deeper, just as in marriage or other relationships. It is the work of "and."

The wisdom tradition is always a subtext, it seems — partially suspect in the eyes of the mainline tradition, which understandably wants to be systematic, reasonable, and defensible to its adversaries.[42] I wonder if this is what Jesus meant when he said, "I am sending you out as lambs among wolves." It is no fun to be defenseless before bad — or even good — people. In fact, one holy Jesuit predicts that Christianity will likely fight its own mystical tradition more than most religions fight theirs, because it has so heavily invested itself in highly rational structures.[43]

Contemplation began its major decline in the fifteenth and sixteenth centuries, and by the time of the European Reformations we were pulled into such defensive/offensive thinking that the new mind largely died out, even in Catholic and Orthodox monasteries. Thank God for the much-needed Protestant Reformation, but as we noted earlier, even the word "protest" says much about the mentality on both sides for the last five hundred years. Unfortunately, this mentality remained largely dualistic, and major reforms seldom proceeded from mystics or reconcilers (John Wesley, George Fox, and Menno Simons being possible exceptions). Too many reformers and too many popes were angry, ideological, or trapped in their heads and their judgments — precisely what contemplation is not.

While most Catholics lost the tradition, too, and many Orthodox and Protestants rediscovered it, the name "catholic" (universal) is helpful and points in the right direction, since it is not inherently separatist or protesting against something. It is the word that the whole Christian Body used for itself in the first thousand years until the first great schism in 1054; henceforth, like after a painful divorce, we were concerned about being "right" — which is what you always have to do when you separate and need to self-justify.

The Enlightenment pretty largely drove the final nails in the coffin of contemplation, because religion became even more oppositional and defensive in its fear of its "new enemies" of rationalism, scientism, and secularism. When you are concerned with either attacking or defending, manipulating or resisting, pushing or pulling, you cannot be contemplative. *When you are preoccupied with enemies, you are always dualistic.* You can take that as axiomatic: in most cases, you become a mirror image of both what you oppose and what you love (see Ephesians 5:14).

Notice that when the "opposition party" accuses Jesus of ignoring important purity codes, and they are "shocked" at his disobedience to the Law or the Sabbath (Matthew 15:12), Jesus does not engage them rationally and try to defeat their argument. In effect, he says to his disciples: Don't bother with them. If it is not of God, it will die of its own dead weight. They are blind, and if you oppose them you will become blind, too, and both of you will fall into the pit (13–14). This is a profound teaching, and a nonviolent one, in a time before there was a word for nonviolence.

I have read we did not have the word "nonviolence" in most Western languages till the 1950s, because we lacked the clear concept of it. This is true in general: you create words only for what you have experienced or can imagine. I suspect and hope it will be the same for nonduality in the century ahead. For some reason, we resist "non" words: Western people want to positively know — and know rationally, which surely narrows the field of knowability!

MORE RECENT REDISCOVERIES

In opposing the ironically named Enlightenment, and thereby becoming oppositional itself, Western Christianity lost its own unique and utterly valid enlightenment. Christianity became rational to oppose rationalism, losing its secret "wisdom," as Paul loved to call it (see 1 Corinthians 1:17–2:16, among other passages). In Europe, this took the form of highly academic theology, and in America the form of narrow ahistorical fundamentalism. Both of these are largely in the head — and the left brain at that — showing little interest in issues such as human suffering, healing, poverty, environmentalism, social justice, inclusivity, care for the outsider, or political oppression. In recent centuries, the Christian churches were on the wrong sides of most human reformations and revolutions, until *after* these reformations succeeded. As a result, Christianity has often become ineffective or even in-credible to much of the world. Our history now works against us.

As Thomas Merton (1910–68) so often did, he makes this point succinctly: "*We are too rational. . . . All that is best is uncon-scious or superconscious.*"[44] Merton, the Cistercian monk based in Kentucky, was not always appreciated by his fellow monks, or the church, in his lifetime. He was too far ahead of his own time, and in his broad knowledge of the tradition, he had access too far back. I would call him *the* American religious prophet of the twentieth century, and very tellingly he was excised from the offi-cial Catholic Catechism by American bishops who viewed him as suspect. Almost singlehandedly in his writings of the 1950s and 1960s, Merton reopened the field, reintroduced the much more traditional vocabulary, and reawakened the true contem-plative mind in the West. Another one of those larger-than-life people!

We are now enjoying the immense fruits of his and others' work, over forty years after his tragic death in 1968. Many others have now built upon his courage in pulling back the curtain and revealing that much of Western religion "has no clothes" — or at least, it has lost its own proper and unique clothing. It largely lost the deeper wisdom tradition that Jesus so ideally taught.[45]

I remember a comment one of the Gethsemani monks made to me during a 1985 retreat I gave them: "Merton told us we were not even contemplatives — we were just introverts!" It must have hurt to hear this, but of course he was largely right. They were good and holy introverts, but often trapped in dualistic thought patterns that must have made their life an unnecessary torture for themselves and one another. I have found the same in many contemplative communities I have visited: some profoundly "get it," and many others are highly frustrated and frustrating people.

Most contemplatives in the last five hundred years were like Teresa of Avila, who says in her autobiography that "she suffered so much because 'thinking prayer' was presented to her as the only form."[46] Not until she discovered the Franciscan Francisco de Osuna, who still understood the older tradition, did she find "her master," as she says.[47] One friar called it the *no pensar nada* or the *pensar sin pensar* method. We had to kneel in silence for twenty minutes each morning in chapel, but no one was trained to teach us how to "think without thinking." We did not know what to do with our minds during that excruciatingly long time. Many of us fell asleep, in more ways than one, and gave up on what we contradictorily called "mental prayer." That is exactly what it was — and what it was not supposed to be. We were victims of our own lost tradition, even of our own great Bonaventure, who taught it clearly.[48] It was there in his writings, but we could not see what we had not been told to see or what our teachers themselves had never experienced.

As long as you understand prayer as merely "thinking holy thoughts" or even "meditating on pious images," you will normally remain in dualistic consciousness. You must be taught to go beyond this, and how it is possible to do so. It was no overstatement for Teresa to call it "suffering," and it was suffering as well for generations of monks and nuns who, in many cases, must have slogged through the thinking prayers by will power, or who for all practical purposes gave up. I have often witnessed this in the lives of fellow monks and nuns today. "Social prayer" took over to partially fill the void. Even today, Catholicism seriously overplays the liturgy card, because it does not know it has a much larger deck available.

This lost tradition continues to this day and is probably why religious orders no longer appear to offer any serious alternative consciousness in society except our celibacy — which, if not practiced well, can actually reinforce dualistic thought. We lost our radical alternativeness, which needs to be at the most foundational level of mind, body, and heart.[49] We cannot rely on society to keep it alive. Today, contemplation is simply too countercultural for most of us who get caught up in that normal world of buying and selling, working, and raising children. As the Scriptures put it, "If we do these things to the green wood, what will happen to the dry?" (Luke 23:32). I have even seen this response to the teaching of Eckhart Tolle. So many knew he was a brilliant spiritual teacher, but most people gave up after a while, saying it was too hard to live in the now.

If it is any consolation, "the whole batch of dough will get it, if a small handful of dough gets it," as Paul says in Romans 11:16. Jesus and Paul loved to use this metaphor of leaven, a truth we now indicate popularly with *the hundredth monkey* or the *tipping point.* God has always been willing to work with a remnant, a critical mass, or what Genesis calls "ten just men." Tipping points and leavening is apparently God's way, a God so humble that she is willing to be an alternative in her own world.

What we are enjoying now, and the hope I wish to offer in this book, is a renaissance of the contemplative mind, the one truly unique alternative that religion has to offer the world.[50] Without this new mind, most doctrines, moralities, dogmas, and church structures will almost certainly be misunderstood, misused, and mishandled. Small people make everything small.

Dualistic people use knowledge, even religious knowledge, for the purposes of ego enhancement, shaming, and the control of others and themselves, for it works very well in that way. Nondual people use knowledge for the transformation of persons and structures, but most especially to change themselves and to see reality with a new eye and heart. They hold and "suffer" the conflicts of life instead of passing them on or projecting them elsewhere. They do not get rid of life's pain until they learn its necessary lessons. Such a holding tank that agrees to hold it all, eliminating nothing, is what I mean by living in the naked now and being present outside the mind.

Do remember this: I am not writing this book to change anybody's beliefs, doctrines, dogmas, or moralities. I am hoping to change *the mind by which you understand those very things*. That will change whatever still needs to be changed, but now Someone Else can do the changing — and we can get back to simply being friends and humans.

CHAPTER FIFTEEN

Faith Is More How to Believe
Than What to Believe

The most beautiful thing we can experience is the mysterious.
It is the source of all true art and all science. He to whom this
"emotion" is a stranger, who can no longer pause to wonder,
or stand rapt in awe, is as good as dead. His eyes are closed.
— ALBERT EINSTEIN, MASTER OF BOTH
DUALISTIC AND NONDUALISTIC THINKING

Like "prayer," "religion," and so many other words, the word
"faith" means different things to different people. As we recover
the lost tradition of contemplation, here are twelve clarifications
for what I mean by "faith" and why, understood in a nondualistic
way, faith is not blind assent, or even reasoned assent, but an
essential part of spiritual transformation.

1. Faith is a word that points to *an initial opening* of the heart
space or the mind space from our side. Initially and foundation-
ally, this is all that faith is, but its effects and implications can be
enormous. Faith is our small but necessary offering to any new
change or encounter.

2. Such an opening or re-opening is entirely necessary to
help you make fresh starts or break through to new levels. You
normally have to let go of the old and go through a stage of
unknowing or confusion, before you can move to another level

of awareness or new capacity. This staging and stepping-over is largely what we mean by faith, and it explains why *doubt and faith are correlative terms*. People of great faith often suffer bouts of great doubt at many levels because they continue to grow at new levels. Mother Teresa experienced decades of this kind of doubt, as was widely reported sometime after her death. The very fact that the world media and people in general so little understood this in her demonstrates how limited is our understanding of the nature of Biblical faith.

3. Such a movement is necessary in all encounters, relationships, or intellectual breakthroughs, not just with the Divine. Human faith and religious faith are much the same except in their object or goal. What set us on the wrong path was making the object of religious faith "ideas" or doctrines instead of a person.[51] Our faith is not a faith that dogmas or moral opinions are true, but a faith that Ultimate Reality/God/Jesus is accessible to us — and even on our side. Jesus was able to touch and heal people who trusted him as an emissary of God's love, not people who assessed intellectual statements and decided whether they were true or false.

4. This movement in faith allows you to bypass your usual pattern of dualistic thinking: not forever, but *just long enough* to think and act holistically — contemplatively — for a while. That is its only point. It is not about believing unbelievable things or renouncing your rational mind. Eventually, you must make use of reason again or, instead of becoming a mystic, you quickly become *mystified!*

5. This contemplative thinking and acting lasts long enough (hopefully) for some form of *mutuality, presence, or mystery* to be "tasted." This in turn leads you on a search for an even deeper

encounter. "All real living is meeting," as Martin Buber says. You cannot be present or meet new reality — *and let it be truly new or itself* — with the judging, dualistic mind. On this point I wholeheartedly agree with Eckhart Tolle in his groundbreaking *The Power of Now,* which puts in contemporary language the older tradition sometimes called "The Sacrament of the Present Moment."[52] The Psalmist said it well in Psalm 34:8: not "think and see" but "taste and see."

6. Once you have gained even momentary access to nondual unity, all previous stages can be returned to as needed, including your dualistic reason. In fact, your reason will have a new freedom and clarity, because it is less needy — it does not need to always be right, self-sufficient, or convinced it possesses the whole picture. Further, if you do not return to "reasonable" language in some sense, your faith is both unshareable and unable to be critiqued by others or even by yourself. (We face this situation today with fundamentalism.) No matter how "mystical" our lives, we must be able to "have our answer ready for those who ask you for the reason for the hope that is within you" (1 Peter 3:15). As Catholic theology has always insisted, faith and reason are not opposites.

7. In fact, the litmus test, the proof that an apparently higher state of awareness is genuinely higher, is that *it always includes and honors all the previous stages.* It is no longer either-or thinking but now both-and thinking, which amounts to an altogether different way of thinking. If this were not true, nondual thinking could itself rightly be accused of being dualistic!

8. Immature religious faith is usually prerational, and has not yet passed through the rings of fire — the "dark nights of purification" — to the transrational. It is what St. Paul refers to as

"milk" instead of spiritual "meat" (1 Corinthians 3:1–2). Most critics and unbelievers think that the transrational person is operating from the prerational mind, yet they are two wholly different stages. Ken Wilber calls this confusion the common "pretrans fallacy." The first stage is necessary and good, but it is also a stage to move *through* if you want to reach adult religion. To stay too long in infantile religion leaves you vulnerable to being easily scandalized, prone to oppositional thinking, defensive, and generally unable to be inclusive, conversational, and respectful with those outside your small circle. What Jesus means by "being a child" is the initial "beginner's mind" and vulnerability we are talking about here. He is not idealizing infantile prerational thinking. From the outside the two can look the same, until you draw close and see that one (the transrational) is free, and the other (the prerational) is either inexperienced or scared, or both.

9. When engaging with one who has *not* gone through the rings of fire, any attempt to "prove" the existence of God — or even the reasonableness of your own faith — will invariably meet with failure. It can be reasonable only to those who have endured the temporary unknowing darkness, the "childhood," and have returned on a different level of awareness. For example, see Paul's own experience: the initial blindness; the scales falling from his eyes, as in Acts 9:9, 18, 20; his retreat in Arabia in Galatians 1:17; and his return transformed. This journey of Paul surely symbolizes the unsayability of faith, and it makes you feel very powerless or foolish around those who have not made the same journey. It also explains Jesus' frequent, bothersome, and surprising line to his disciples and beneficiaries: "Don't tell anyone!" No doubt, this was hard for them to hear. But often, to try to talk about the

unsayable to the "crowds" is to trivialize it, or even to lose its depth, like describing great lovemaking to an outsider.

10. Many of the "cultured despisers of religion" are therefore right in what they are suspicious of, which is usually the immature form of religion, a form that is largely dominant today. They are attacking the "what" that we claim to know, whereas *the mature believer is primarily claiming a different way of knowing* — the "how" that allows her to see many more things. True God experience is a compelling Presence and an Inner Aliveness that serves for better seeing. (Think of the difference a pair of night goggles makes for those attempting to see in the dark.) This is deeper than what the critics of religion attack, deeper than any mere psychological state or childhood religious conditioning, which tend to be *rigid* and *fragile*. You can tell adult and authentic faith by people's ability to deal with darkness, failure, and nonvalidation of the ego — and by their quiet but confident joy! Infantile religion insists on certitudes or "light" every step of the way and thus is not very happy.

11. Fortunately, in every age, country, denomination, institution, diocese, and monastery there is invariably a leavening remnant who understands this. You sometimes wonder how they got there. No religion, denomination, or lifestyle has a monopoly here. This is self-evident even by recalling Paul's well-known list of the fruits of the Spirit in Galatians 5:22, which can be found across the boundaries of culture and religion. If not, it is indeed a "field of dry bones" (Ezekiel 37), and little new or good will happen there.

12. This is surely why most spiritual teachers advise some form of "faith," although they use different words for the same idea. Jesus praises faith even more than love. "Your faith has

saved you" is often his concluding word, as in Luke 8:48. Why? Because typically, wisdom, love, or further growth will not go deeper without *another* opening up or letting go, and for some reason, each time you have to learn it again and "reopen." Faith is more a breaking-through, which then allows you to hold on — precisely because now Someone is holding on to you! Faith enlightens the path behind you, but as a rule, in front of you it is still dark. Now, however, not so threatening or impossible, because for you "a light shines on in the darkness, and the darkness cannot overpower it" (John 1:5).

Who are the people of every place and time who have discovered this deeper meaning of faith in the midst of darkness? Almost without exception, they are those who have suffered much or loved deeply. Those two experiences are the common crossover points, the rings of fire, and because love and suffering are available to all, the eyes of true faith are available to all. We look at these crossover points now.

CHAPTER SIXTEEN

Opening the Door
Great Love and Great Suffering

For love is as strong as death,
The flash of it is a flash of fire,
A flame of Yahweh Himself
— Song of Songs 8:6

All humans born of women have a short life,
and it is full of suffering. — Job 14:1

Two universal and prime paths of transformation have been available to every human being God has created since Adam and Eve and the Stone Age: great love and great suffering. These are offered to all; they level the playing fields of all the world religions. Only love and suffering are strong enough to break down our usual ego defenses, crush our dual thinking, and open us up to Mystery. In my experience, they like nothing else exert the mysterious chemistry that can transmute us from a fear-based life into a love-based life. None of us are exactly sure why. We do know that words, even good words or totally orthodox theology, cannot achieve that by itself. No surprise that the Christian icon of redemption is a man offering love from a crucified position.

Love and suffering are a part of most human lives. Without doubt, *they are the primary spiritual teachers* more than any

Bible, church, minister, sacrament, or theologian. Wouldn't it make sense for God to make divine truth so available? If the love of God is as perfect and victorious as we believe, wouldn't it offer every human equal and universal access to the Divine as love and suffering do? This is what Paul seems to be saying to the pagan Athenians in his brilliant sermon on the Acropolis: "All can seek the Deity, feeling their way toward him and succeeding in finding him. For God is not far from any of us, since it is in God that we live and move and have our being" (Acts 17:27–28). What a brilliant, and needed, piece of theology to this day.

Love is what we long for and were created for — in fact, love is what we *are* as an outpouring from God — but suffering often seems to be our opening to that need, that desire, and that identity. Love and suffering are the main portals that open up the mind space and the heart space (either can come first), breaking us into breadth and depth and communion. Almost without exception, great spiritual teachers will always have strong direct guidance about love and suffering. If you never go there, you will not know the essentials. You'll try to work it all out in your head, but your mind alone can't get you there. You must "love with your whole heart, your whole soul, your whole mind, and your whole strength" (Mark 12:30), or it does not appear to be love at all. That's how love works and why it leads to the giving up of control, which is my simple definition of suffering: *whenever you are not in control.*

When you are inside of great love and great suffering, you have a much stronger possibility of surrendering your ego controls and opening up to the whole field of life. Frankly, because you do not have much choice now, you are being led. Great love makes you willing to risk everything, holding nothing back. The feeling of fusion or acceptance by another, or with the Other, at least temporarily overcomes your terrible sense of aloneness, separateness, and fear. The ecstasy of this union makes you let down your barriers and *see things inside of a new kind of wholeness and happiness for a while.* Love songs in every language are celebrating this wondrous experience, almost as if there was nothing else in the world to sing about.

No wonder people run toward love. At least for a while, one's seeing is much broader, more adventuresome, and less defensive. But love can never be sustained at this honeymoon level for long. This is surely one reason for such strong taboos against promiscuity, solo sex, or premarital sex in most religions. Such behavior can easily trivialize, make ordinary, or even make impossible this temporary ecstatic seeing and this crucial opening of the heart space. (We are seeing this on a broad global level today with the easy access to Internet pornography, where no opening of the heart is needed.) To sustain this wondrous open heart long-term, and to remain permanently "in love," something else is needed — some level of mysticism, whether nature-based, consciousness-based, or God-based.

Great suffering opens you in a different way. Here, things happen *against your will* — which is what makes it suffering. And over time, you can learn to give up your defended state, again because you have no choice. *The situation is what it is,* although we will invariably go through the stages of denial, anger, bargaining, resignation, and (hopefully) on to acceptance. The suffering might feel wrong, terminal, absurd, unjust, impossible, physically painful, or just outside of your comfort zone. So you see why we must have a proper attitude toward suffering, because many things every day leave us out of control — even if just a long stoplight. Remember always, however, that *if you do not transform your pain, you will surely transmit it to those around you and even to the next generation.*

Suffering, of course, can lead you in either of two directions: It can make you very bitter and close you down, or it can make you wise, compassionate, and utterly open, either because your heart has been softened, or perhaps because suffering makes you feel like you have nothing more to lose. It often takes you to the edge of your inner resources where you "fall into the hands of the living God" (Hebrews 10:31), even against your will. We must all pray for the grace of this second path of softening and opening. My personal opinion is that this is the very meaning of the phrase "deliver us from evil" in the Our Father (Lord's Prayer). We aren't asking to avoid suffering. It is as if we were praying, "When the big trials come, God, hold on to me, and don't let me turn bitter or blaming," an evil that leads to so many other evils.

Struggling with one's own shadow self, facing interior conflicts and moral failures, undergoing rejection and abandonment, daily humiliations, experiencing any kind of abuse, or any form of limitation: all are gateways into deeper consciousness and the flowering of the soul. These experiences give us a privileged window into the naked now, because impossible contradictions are staring us in the face. Much needed healing, forgiving what is, "weeping over" and accepting one's interior poverty and contradictions are normally necessary experiences to invite a person into the contemplative mind. (Watch Paul do this in a classic way from the depths of Romans 7:14 to the heights of his mystic poetry in most of Romans 8.)

In facing the contradiction that we ourselves are, we become living icons of both/and. Once you can accept mercy, it is almost natural to hand it on to others (see the story of the unforgiving debtor in Matthew 18:23–35). You become a conduit of what you yourself have received. If you have never needed mercy and do not face your own inherent contradictions, you can go from youth to old age, dualistically locked inside a mechanistic universe. That, in my opinion, is the "sin against the Holy Spirit." It cannot be forgiven because there is a refusal to recognize that you even need mercy or forgiveness. You have blocked the conduit that you are. Did you ever notice the remarkable fact that in her great Magnificat Mary speaks three times of God showing her "mercy"? (Luke 2:49, 54, 55) If even the Virgin Mary, the Mother of Jesus, lives under that mercy, how much more so the rest of us?

Great love has the potential to open the heart space and then the mind space. Great suffering has the potential to open the mind space, and then the heart space. Eventually, both spaces need to be opened, and for such people nondual thinking can be the easiest. People who have never loved or never suffered will normally try to control everything with an either-or attitude, or all-or-nothing thinking. This closed system is all they're prepared for. The mentality that divides the world into "deserving and undeserving" has never been let go of by any experience of grace or undeserved mercy. This absence leaves them judgmental, demanding, unforgiving, and weak in empathy and sympathy. They remain inside of the prison of meritocracy, where all has to be deserved. Remember, however, to be patient with such people, even if you are the target of their judgment, because on some level that is how they treat themselves as well.

Authentic love is of one piece. How you love anything is how you love everything. Jesus commands us to "Love our neighbors *as* we love ourselves," and he connects the two great commandments of love of God and love of neighbor, saying they are "like" one another (Matthew 22:40). So often, we think this means to love our neighbor with the same amount of love — *as much as* we love ourselves — when it really means that it is the same Source and the same Love that allows me to love myself, and others, and God — at the same time! That is unfortunately not the way most people understand love, compassion, and forgiveness, but it is the only way they ever work. *How you love is how you have accessed Love.*

You cannot sincerely love another or forgive another's offenses inside of dualistic consciousness. Try it, and you'll see it can't be done. We have done the people of God a great disservice by preaching the Gospel to them but not giving them the tools whereby they can obey that Gospel. As Jesus put it, "Cut off from the vine, you can do nothing" (John 15:5). The "vine and the branches" are one of the greatest Christian mystical images of the nonduality between God and the soul. In and with God, I can love everything and everyone — even my enemies. Alone and by myself, will power and intellect will seldom be able to love in difficult situations over time. Many sophisticated folks try to love by themselves. They try to obey the second commandment without the first. It usually does not work long-term, and there is no one more cynical than a disillusioned idealist. (This was my own youthful generation of the 1960s.)

Finally, of course, there is a straight line between love and suffering. If you love greatly, it is fairly certain you will soon suffer, because you have somehow given up control to another.

Undoubtedly, this is why we are told to be faithful in our loves, because such long-term loyalty will always lead us to the necessary pruning (John 15:2) of the narcissistic self.

> Until we love and until we suffer, we all try to figure out life and death with our minds, but afterward a Larger Source opens up within us and we "think" and feel quite differently: "Until knowing the Love, which is beyond all knowledge" (Ephesians 3:19). Thus Jesus would naturally say something like, "This is my commandment, you *must* love one another!" (John 13:34). Love, I believe, is the only way to initially and safely open the door of awareness and aliveness, and then *suffering for that love* keeps that door open and available for ever greater growth. They are the two great doors, and we dare not leave them closed.

PART THREE

CHAPTER SEVENTEEN

What Nondual Thinking Is Not

From now on, we must look at nothing from the ordinary point of view. If anyone is in Christ, they have become a completely new construct, and the old construct must pass away!   — 2 CORINTHIANS 5:16 (MY PARAPHRASE)

We divide in thought what is undivided in nature.
     — ALAN WATTS, *The Two Hands of God*

When we come from a dualistic mind, we can conceive of anything, including nondualism, only dualistically. With experiences such as love and suffering, we gradually come to understand the contemplative gaze in a different way. For our divided mind, however, it's helpful to remove a few misconceptions. What is nondual thinking *not?*

- Nondual thinking is not "relativism."

- It is not skepticism.

- It is not merely saying "There are two sides to everything."

- It is not merely admitting that there are different perspectives in any situation.

- It is not fuzzy thinking.

- It is not a refusal to place your bet.

- It is not an esoteric Eastern philosophy.

- It is not postmodern nihilism.

- It is not an avoidance of appropriate judgments.

In fact, nondual thinking or contemplation is a sign that you have found the Absolute, but it is far beyond any words or ideas. A new "Law" puts all other laws and criteria into an utterly new perspective. This is the dangerous freedom Paul is talking about in Galatians 3 and 5. Only some kind of authentic God experience, or True Transcendence, grounds you in nonduality. Why? Because you have encountered the One, God, or naked Being Itself, which breaks open and is beyond all mental and expected boundaries. Despite their differences, both John Duns Scotus and Thomas Aquinas said that *Deus est Ens,* "God is being itself." This is not some novel idea from Asia, but a forgotten truth of Christian history. Such being has no boundaries that the mind can conceive. Or as our Franciscan St. Bonaventure put it, "God is the One whose center is everywhere and whose circumference is nowhere." It takes a different mind to live in such a different space and time.

For saints, mystics, and budding contemplatives, "words have become flesh," and experience has gone beyond words. Experience is always nondual, an open field. As St. Paul put it, "my spirit is praying, but my mind is left barren" (1 Corinthians 14:14). Words are mere guideposts now, and you recognize that most people have made them into hitching posts. Inside of such broad and deep awareness, paradoxes are easily accepted, and former mental contradictions seem to dissolve. That's why mystics can forgive and let go and show mercy and love enemies.

Only abstract concepts and verbal dogmas contain the air of mathematical or divine perfection, but mystics do not primarily love concepts. They have had at least one significant encounter with the Divine, which is all it takes, and which they themselves cannot understand or describe in a clear concept. "There is only Christ: he is everything and he is in everything" (Colossians 3:11), they might say. To the outsider, it sounds like overstatement or mere poetry, but afterward, such people are not rebels against anything except any attempts to block that kind of encounter for others. They are only in love, with life, and life for all. They may look dangerous and even heretical to those who have not shared a similar experience, and that is a burden they must forever carry. They have no time for being against; *there is now so much to be for!*

Nondual thinking is a way of seeing that refuses to eliminate the negative, the problematic, the threatening parts of everything. It rejects any way that too quickly says, "That is not possible!" or "That does not make sense!" As such, nondual thinking actually clarifies and sharpens your rational mind and increases your ability to see truthfully because your biases and fears are out of the way. Nondual thinking does not divide the field of the naked now, nor does it eliminate the problematic, but receives it all. This demands some degree of real detachment from yourself. The nondual/contemplative mind holds truth humbly, knowing that if it is true, it is its own best argument, and any formulation is still partial and "imperfect," as Paul says in 1 Corinthians 13:12.

The contemplative knows that truth held arrogantly will not bear the wonderful fruit of truth. Moral outrage at the ideas of others hardly ever serves God's purposes, only our own.

Non-polarity thinking (if you prefer that phrase) teaches you how to hold creative tensions, how to live with paradox and contradictions, how not to run from mystery, and therefore how to actually practice what all religions teach as necessary: compassion, mercy, loving kindness, patience, forgiveness, and humility. It allows you to live in the naked now and to resist the pulls toward any shameful past or any idyllic future. One wonders if these virtues are even possible in any other way.

At the present maturity level of most mass religion, we have largely been taught the opposite. We judgmentally look for the sin, error, or mistake in ourselves or others, not to consider its message for us, but to catch it, hate it, eliminate it, and often to project it elsewhere. Such people easily "see the splinter in their neighbor's eye, while unable to see the log in their own" (Matthew 7:3), as Jesus put it. The problem is endemic among many religious types. *What you resist persists,* but now in a disguised form — and inside of you. Only then can I begin to understand what Jesus probably meant by "resist not evil" (Matthew 5:39). My dualistic mind thought it utterly irresponsible on his part to suggest this, but now I can see that Jesus was a psychological genius. James seems to be saying the same as well: "The person of two minds will be unstable in all that they do" (1:8).

We are saying here, as religion historically did, that you need a whole new "head" (as in Romans 12:2). You need a new motherboard, changing the actual hardware that processes your experiences. It is not merely a change of morals, group affiliation, or belief systems, but a change at the very heart of the way that you receive, hear, and pass on your own experience. This is transformative religion. We need true sanctity if this world is to thrive and Christianity is to be something more than a protector of privilege, fear-based thinking, and the status quo. We need what Paul calls "a new mind," which is the result of a "spiritual revolution" (Ephesians 4:23).

The dualistic mind gives us sanity and safety, and that is good enough. But to address our religious and social problems in any creative or finally helpful way, we also need something more, something bigger, and something much better.[53] We need "the mind of Christ."

(1 Corinthians 2:16)

CHAPTER EIGHTEEN

The Watchful Gaze

What Do We Mean by Being "Awake"?

How can one understand that part of you which does the
understanding? — UPANISHADS, II, 4, 14

Religious teachers, including Jesus, the Buddha, as well as many
Hindu sages, are always telling us to wake up — to be alert, alive,
awake, attentive, or aware. You might call it the AAAAA recov-
ery program! But how can you do that? What does *being awake*
actually mean?

- Does it mean being happy?

- Does it mean thinking about things more?

- Does it mean doing more good and reasonable thinking?

- Does it mean being grateful and appreciative?

- Does it mean being helpful and useful with what is right in
  front of you?

- Does it mean not wasting time and being more productive?

- Does it mean trying harder and doing better?

- Does it mean reflecting regularly — what Catholics call the
  daily examination of conscience?

In my gatherings, these are the most common ways that people understand the phrase, and they might well be some of the good *results* of being awake. But they are not the essential insight. This is *not* what the great traditions mean by paying attention, being conscious, or being awake. It is quite important to understand this.

Being conscious or aware means:

- I drop to a level deeper than the passing show.

- I become the calm seer of my dramas from that level.

- I watch myself compassionately from a little distance, almost as if the "myself" is someone else — "a corpse," as St. Francis put it.

- I dis-identify with my own emotional noise, and no longer let it pull me here and there, up and down.

- I stop thinking about this or that and "collapse into" pure consciousness of nothing in particular. You don't *get* there, you *fall* there — "objectless consciousness," as some call it.

At first, it does not feel like "me," and is even unfamiliar territory, because up to now I thought that my thinking was "me," yet now my thinking has ceased. This is the accurate meaning of Jesus' teaching on "losing oneself to find oneself" in Luke 9:24.

This new and broader sense of "me" soon begins to feel like your deepest and truest self; it seems solid and unchanging. At this point God, consciousness, me, silent emptiness, and fullness (at the same time) all start to feel like the same wonderful thing!

I believe this deeper self is what most traditions were referring to as "the soul" or the True Self, and what some might call "the collective unconscious," because when you live there you are somehow "shared" and participating in Something Larger. You are not doing it; it is being done to you. (Paradoxically, this pure consciousness is usually described as the "unconscious," because we are in a sense not at home there at all.)

This new perspective and foundation allows me to see things for what they really are — and also for what they are not at all. It is indeed a radical perceptual shift that the tradition would call conversion.

I can then begin to enjoy all things in themselves, and not in terms of their usefulness or importance or threat to me. This "I," this "little ol' me," stops being the significant reference point for anything. (Nothing else deserves to be called freedom except this foundational freedom from the self, which is why even imprisoned people and physically limited people can be utterly free.)

This awareness deepens gradually on the cellular level, breathing level, heart level, seeing level, hearing level, touching level, aroma level. This is what is being refined in a regular contemplative "sit." The thinking level will be the last to "fall" because it always overstates its own importance and represses the other sources. So you must practice ignoring it.

I can then later move in to change, fix, or do what needs to be done, but *I do not have to do so in order to be content or happy.* This shift changes the entire situation much more than you might at first imagine. Now there is not much room for compulsivity, fanaticism, trumped-up excitement, or even depression. Equanimity is the very nature of the soul. Jesus would have called it "the peace the world cannot give, nor take away" (John 14:27).

I no longer use events or titles, roles or opinions, clothing or money, affiliations or contacts, or even churches, temples, or synagogues to define myself. I make good "use" of them, and can also let go of them or even keep them and love them, but I do not "believe" them as if they represented final substantial reality. They are all passing, relative goods.

I stop labeling, ranking, and categorizing people and things and just *see* them; typically, this will lead to a quiet joy and deep peace and contentment. This is presence, or what Simone Weil would call "absolute attention."

I am no longer emotionally jerked around by things that do not matter. (If I am personally *identified* with my private viewing platform, every event has the power to snag and control me.)

If I cannot detach from a person or event or feeling when it is needed or appropriate, then I can take it as certain that I am overidentified, overly attached, or even enmeshed. This could be called unawareness, the unawakened state, or blindness. Seemingly, this is true of most people, because no one ever told them there was another way.

I am now on a solid viewing platform, apart from the usual level of small self, where I can see things as God might see them. This is the beginning of nondual thinking and is surely "the mind of Christ" that Paul says we can participate in (1 Corinthians 2:16), or the "mental revolution" that leads to an utterly new self (Ephesians 4:23–24).

When this happens to you, you are now a living paradox: at one and the same time utterly connected to everybody else in a compassionate and caring way, and absolutely free to be *your own self.* Your identity comes from within. You will want to love and serve others, but you do not use them or need them to define yourself either positively or negatively. This is surely

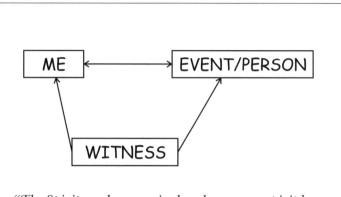

"The Spirit you have received and your own spirit bear UNITED WITNESS, and what you can then see is that you are a part of God, and God is a part of you," and you now see this from a new united eye!

— A summary and paraphrase of Romans 8:14–16

- Meditators and Buddhists would call this the "Stable Witness," which is attained by discipline and practice, leading to "realization" of union with Being Itself.

- Christians would call it the indwelling Holy Spirit, which is "realized" primarily by surrender to and trust of a divine union that is already given. You will, however, need discipline to keep seeing and trusting this Union, because of the pressure and seduction of all the contrary evidence.

- "This Spirit will teach you all things and *'re-mind'* you of all that I taught you." (John 14:26) "the freedom and glory of the children of God" (Romans 8:21). Such people know how to love *you* very well, because *they* are out of the way.

The aware mind allows you to enjoy *the inherent aliveness* in all things, and in yourself, before things and people are categorized or deemed worthy or unworthy, important or unimportant.

This mystical seeing is the "thinking without thinking" of the older tradition (Fray Francisco de Osuna — *pensar sin pensar* and *no pensar nada*).

This is identification with the awareness behind thought, consciousness itself, pure being, or the perspective of "the soul."

This is the beginnings of joy, and sometimes even the joy that Jesus calls "complete" (John 15:11).

This is the fulfillment of Socrates' "Know Thyself," yet much deeper than any mere psychological knowing of your personality traits or motivations.

This is the Third Eye, the eye of the True Self.
This is what it means to pay attention and to access the Source.
This is contemplation and dwelling in the naked now.
And it is available always and everywhere,
It is available to you, now.

CHAPTER NINETEEN

The Meaning of Spiritual Love

When you regarded me
Your eyes imprinted your grace in me,
In this, you loved me again,
And thus my eyes merited
To also love what you see in me....
Let us go forth together to see ourselves in Your beauty.
— St. John of the Cross, *Spiritual Canticle,* 32, 33

When we read poetry as beautiful and profound as this verse, we can see why John of the Cross was far ahead of his time in the spiritual and psychological understanding of how love works and how true love changes us at a deep level. He consistently speaks of divine love as the template and model for all human love, and human love as the necessary school and preparation for any transcendent encounter. *If you have never experienced human love, it will be very hard for you to access God as Love. If you have never let God love you, you will not know how to love humanly in the deepest way.* Of course, grace can overcome both of these limitations. In this surely inspired passage, John describes the very process of love at its best:

You give a piece of yourself *to* the other.
You see a piece of yourself *in* the other (usually unconsciously).

This allows the other to do the same in return.
You do not need or demand anything back from them,
because you know that you are both participating
in a single, Bigger Gazing and Loving —
one that fully satisfies and creates an immense Inner
　　Aliveness.
(Simply to love is its own reward.)
You accept being accepted — for no reason and by no criteria
　　whatsoever!
This is the key that unlocks everything in me, for others,
　　and toward God.
So much so that we call it "salvation"!

To put it another way, what I let God see and accept in me
also becomes what I can then see and accept in myself. And even
more, it becomes that whereby I see everything else. This is "radical grace." This is why it is crucial to allow God, and at least one
other person, to see us in our imperfection and even our naked-
ness, as we are — rather than as we would ideally wish to be. It
is also why we must give others this same experience of being
looked upon in *their* imperfection; otherwise, they will never
know the essential and utterly transformative mystery of grace.
This is the glue that binds the universe of persons together.

Such utterly free and gratuitous love is the only love that
validates, transforms, and changes us at the deepest levels of consciousness. It is what we all desire and what we were created for.
Once you allow it for yourself, you will almost naturally become
a conduit of the same for others. In fact, nothing else will attract
you anymore or even make much sense.

Can you let God "look upon you in your lowliness," as Mary put it in Luke 1:47, without waiting for some future moment when you believe you are worthy? Remember the words of John of the Cross: "Love what God sees in you." Many of us never go there, because to be loved in this way is to live in the naked now, and it is indeed a quite naked moment.

CHAPTER TWENTY

Sinners, Mystics, and Astrophysicists
How to Celebrate Paradox

All that is hidden and all that is plain I have come to know through Wisdom. Within her is a spirit intelligent, unique, manifold, subtle, active, incisive, lucid, invulnerable, benevolent, dependable, unperturbed, all seeing.... She pervades and permeates all things, she is the untarnished mirror of God's active power. She is one, and makes all things new, and in each generation passes into holy souls.

— WISDOM 7:21–27

By and large Western civilization is a celebration of the illusion that good may exist without evil, light without darkness, and pleasure without pain, and this is true of both its Christian and secular technological phases.

— ALAN WATTS, *The Two Hands of God*

Once after a spirituality conference in California where I had spoken, a rather assertive listener came up to me and said, "Richard, you appear to be an intelligent man. You don't really believe all that stuff, do you? All those doctrines and dogmas of the church? Most Christians look like Walt Disney in Fantasyland, and on LSD at that!" I am sure the man was being sincere and trying to help me or free me from what he thought was imprisonment.

I told him that I indeed did believe the major doctrines of the tradition, and that I bet he would, too, if he just had the right pair of glasses and enough inner experience. I told him that I was not there to change anyone's dogmas, but only the eyes with which they understand those dogmas — which, in the eyes of people who have no inner experience, means to radically change the dogmas. I suspect that is why many transformed people are killed by someone from their own group. They think you have been disloyal to the group, when very often you are exhibiting profound loyalty to it.

THE VALUE OF PARADOX

These new eyes have everything to do with seeing and thinking paradoxically — grasping the truth of something that seems a contradiction. Even the great dogmas of the church are almost always totally paradoxical. Think of Jesus = human and divine, Mary = Virgin and Mother, God = 1 and 3, Eucharist = bread and Jesus. Because paradox undermines dual thinking at its very root, the dualistic mind immediately attacks paradox as weak thinking or confusion, separate from hard logic. The very modern phenomenon of fundamentalism shows an almost complete incapacity to deal with paradox, and shows how much we have regressed. But today, thank God, what mystics have always known, great scientists now teach as well, and the church is trying to catch up after a long amnesia.

The history of spirituality tells us that we must learn to accept paradoxes, or we will never love anything or see it correctly. The above passage personifying Wisdom (*Sophia*) is an insightful description of how one sees things paradoxically and contemplatively. Interestingly enough, Scripture calls this subtle seeing "she," which in a patriarchal culture is a way of saying "alternative." Alan Watts says that the loss of paradoxical thinking is the great blindness of our civilization, which is what many of us believe happened when we repressed the feminine side of our lives as the inferior side. It was a loss of all subtlety, discrimination, and capacity for complementarity.

Each one of us must learn to *live with* paradox, or we cannot live peacefully or happily even a single day of our lives. In fact, we must even learn to *love* paradox, or we will never be wise, forgiving, or possessing the patience of good relationships. It is a shame that we should have to assert such an obvious thing. "Untarnished mirrors," as Wisdom says, receive the whole picture, which is always both the darkness, the light, and the subtle shadings of light that make shape, form, color, and texture beautiful. You cannot see in total light or total darkness. You must have variances of light to see. The *shadowlands* are the only world we live in.

Reality *is* paradoxical. If we are honest, everything is a clash of contradictions, and there is nothing on this created earth that is not a mixture at the same time of good and bad, helpful and unhelpful, endearing and maddening, living and dying. St. Augustine called this the "paschal mystery." Even Jesus, the Christ, said to the flattering and rich young man, "Why do you call me good? God alone is good!" (Mark 10:18). Start with your own spouse or children — or yourself. We are all, without exception, a mixed blessing. No pope can deny this, nor does Scripture need to declare it. Paradox is hidden and obvious, everywhere and always — unless you have repressed one side of your very being.

For now, I will offer a simple definition of how I understand paradox: *a paradox is something that initially appears to be inconsistent or contradictory, but might not be a contradiction at all inside of a different frame or seen with a different eye.* I believe that one of religion's main tasks was to give us that eye for paradox and mystery, which the above passage from the Book of Wisdom calls "one." Wisdom sees things all at once and does not divide the field. Wisdom is never just mine, but always a shared experience. Believers would say it is a participation in the very life of God. Wisdom is inherently shared — the Holy Spirit, the collective unconscious, if you will. You or I can never possess wisdom, but merely share in it. We are all plagiarists when it comes to wisdom, which is why I personally never insist on copyrights on my books or recordings (although my publishers do!). We all learned everything from somebody else.

Most of the major teachings of the great religions do not demand blind faith as much as they demand new eyes. To the uninitiated, this demand always looks like blind faith, but it is in fact a different kind of light that allows — or creates — and even appreciates the shadows. Such light allows a compassionate, full, and patient reading of reality. It is often poets who see the truth and can communicate it best. I think of names such as Dante, Shakespeare, Goethe, Dickinson, Hopkins, Rilke, Wordsworth, Walt Whitman, Mary Oliver, Brendan Kennelly, T. S. Eliot, Naomi Nye, Denise Levertov, David Whyte. Without intending disrespect, I note that such wisdom figures have frequently offered the world much more helpful truth than many ecclesiastics, who too often merely reflect what the masses are ready to need and to believe from them.

Western Christianity *has tended to objectify paradoxes in dog-matic statements that demand mental agreement instead of any inner experience of the mystery revealed.*[54] At least we "worship" these paradoxes in the living collision of opposites we call Jesus, which is good. But this approach tends not to give people the underlying principle that Jesus, the Christ, has come to teach us about life and about ourselves. Jesus, as the icon of Christ Consciousness (1 Corinthians 2:16), is the very template of total paradox: human yet divine, heavenly yet earthly, physical yet spiritual, possessing a male body yet a female soul, killed yet alive, powerless yet powerful, victim yet victor, failure yet redeemer, marginalized yet central, singular yet everyone, incarnate yet cosmic, nailed yet liberated, resolving the great philosophical problem of the one and the many. And we made this momentous and cosmic Christ into the private savior of our personal agendas.

Too often teachers gave Christians the brief advice, "Believe in Jesus!" without the great cosmic mystery Jesus actually reveals and without the invitation and call *to see the same truth in ourselves and all of creation.* Jesus is the microcosm of the macrocosm, which might be one way to describe how he "saves" us. What we will not capitulate to, the Christ totally "recapitulates" within himself (Colossians 1:15–20), naming it as true and possible "for all and in all" (1 Corinthians 15:28). This is surely why Jesus keeps saying "Follow me." Jesus is not just the unique son of God, but the public beginning of the great parade of all who are partners with him "in his triumphal procession," as Paul beautifully calls it (2 Corinthians 2:14).[55]

Take this as a Christian axiom: (1) All statements and beliefs about Jesus are also statements about the journey of the soul (birth, chosenness, ordinary life, initiation, career, misunderstanding and opposition, failure, death in several forms, resurrection, and return to God). (2) All statements about "the Christ" are statements about the "Body" of Christ, too. We are not the historical Jesus, but we are the Body of Christ. "Christ" is not Jesus' last name, but the field of communion that includes all of us with him. You do not "believe" these doctrines; you *know* them. They are realizations and personal life experiences. Here, there is nothing to rationally prove or disprove, believe or unbelieve. If you go on a sincere inner journey, you will know them for yourself on some level. Doctrines and dogmas are very good pointers in the right directions. But often it is easier for people to believe things, or even to be moral, than to go on such full and risky journeys. Church doctrines are brilliant and much-needed if we experience the necessary change of mental structure that underlies these very "mysteries." Otherwise, they are largely harmless affirmations.[56] If we do not experience this underlying revelation, what becomes of these sacred, transrational teachings? As we've discussed, religion ends up looking like prerational silliness or merely early life conditioning. Yet God is at work in those lives, too, in a surely unique way, for nothing is ever lost in the great undeserved economy of grace.

Just as those who love and those who suffer are often better able to be open to the letting-go needed for contemplative growth, there are two groups who have a head start in this paradoxical seeing: sinners and mystics. The sinners cannot deny their contradictions, and the mystics, *who go on interior journeys with God,* learn how to face and hold the contradictions, and even weep and laugh over them, as they gradually become a larger "holding tank."[57] Both sinners and mystics have the common experience of having to hold together the contradictory opposites of life. The sinners have had their superiority system grabbed from them. The mystics willingly give up any sense of superiority or separation as they gaze upon the Loving Vision (although this letting go comes not without struggle and many deaths to their illusions).

GREEK LOGIC

Let's address any intellectual resistance you might still have in this way. The way we think and the way intelligent prose works in Western languages is founded on three simple principles of logic that can be found already in Greek philosophy. They are sequential and linear:

1. *The Law of Identity:* A=A. A thing is the same as itself (and no two things are exactly the same).

2. *The Law of Contradiction:* If A=A, then A cannot be B (that which is not A).

3. *The Law of the Excluded Middle or Third:* A cannot be both A and B at the same time.

These principles are at work in all educated Western people, consciously or not; you don't have to know them consciously to follow them. They served us well in terms of the scientific and industrial revolutions, in terms of measurements and math, and most day-to-day life, but their severe limitations in other areas, such as science, philosophy, theology, and astrophysics — are now becoming apparent. We need a way through and a way beyond this closed system. Of itself, Greek logic cannot lead us to the kind of wisdom we are seeking, as Paul himself warned us in 1 Corinthians 1:19–31.

In fact, these Greek principles of logic are reductionistic and not always true at all. They lead to what Ken Wilber calls "flatland." Let's consider two examples of the shortcomings of such logic. One came from fourth-century Christian theology and the other from recent developments in quantum physics and astrophysics. They all undercut and overcome Greek logic and place us inside of a new frame different from what most of us took as self-evident. They are opening up an entirely different mind, and if religion does not wake up, it will, in the centuries to come, find itself even less able to talk to the world.

TRINITY

Trinitarian theology was almost made to order to humiliate the logical Greek mind: It said, in effect: the Father is the Father, but the Father is also the Son, and in fact, he is the Father and the Son at the same time, which relationship is, in fact, the Holy Spirit. If actually encountered and meditated on, the doctrine of God as Trinity breaks down the binary system of the mind.[58] For a Christian who lives in a Trinitarian spirituality, it makes either-or thinking totally useless. Perhaps, in addition to everything else, the Trinity is a blessing, to make us patient before Mystery and to humble our dualistic minds. I noted earlier how the unspeakable name of the Jewish God, YHWH, was supposed to have had the same effect.

Unfortunately, for the majority of Trinitarian Christians, we believed the doctrine of Trinity as some kind of strange riddle, a mathematical conundrum, but never let it call our addiction to

Greek logic into question. The sweet Irish nuns who taught me wisely said, "Don't think about it!" and held up the shamrock as a rather lovely natural symbol of the three-in-one. Even though the doctrine of the Trinity was at the very center of Christian faith, we did not allow it to change our consciousness. We just believed it to be true, and then shelved it, as we did most doctrines. Only the mystics tended to relate to God in a Trinitarian way, and often passionately so (such as Augustine, Bonaventure, Julian of Norwich, and the Cappadocian Fathers). I am certain that the future of Christian mysticism will be strongly Trinitarian, which, perhaps surprisingly, also creates a huge opening for interreligious dialogue. Unfortunately, faith became a matter of believing impossible or strange things (which was supposed to please God, somehow), instead of an entranceway into a very different way of knowing altogether.

We Catholics frequently signed our bodies with the Trinitarian sign of the cross and fully accepted the mental doctrine, but we set it aside as of no practical or real consequence. *We did not let the principle of three undo our dualistic principle of two.* As Karl Rahner taught, we could drop the doctrine of the Trinity tomorrow, and it would have little or no practical effect on the lives of most Christians. This was a real loss and mistake, especially considering that Jesus himself knew no Greek, and clearly did not think with this kind of logic when it came to matters divine.

PHYSICS AND ASTROPHYSICS

Our modern and postmodern world has given our minds any number of recent humiliations, available to all, whether scientists or laypeople, who dare to study atoms, galaxies, and the nature of space and time. One that comes to mind — or better, one that is unable to come to mind — is the discovery that an electron is an impossible mixture of "here" (A) and "there" (B). And at the same time! Any intelligent person would think he is showing his intelligence by saying "Impossible!" It looks like it must be some magic show or an illusionist's trick, but in fact, the "principle of the excluded middle" shows itself not to be true here either. There *is* a third something, although we have no idea how to understand it. We only know it indirectly, by its effects. Something like Spirit!

Quantum physics and astrophysics are filled with similar "logical" impossibilities.[59] Much of the universe seems to feed on paradox and the mysterious — everything from black holes to dark matter to neutrinos, which are invisible and weightless and yet necessary to keep matter and anti-matter from canceling out one another. They have to be there — things don't make sense otherwise — but no one can prove it, because the scientific method cannot measure it or know it, except by its effects.

We have all heard how light is both a wave and a particle, and scientists long ago gave up trying to prove it was just one or the other. It is clearly both — and at the same time! Now how do you deal with facts of that nature, if you are intelligent? This signals that you need a very different kind of intelligence. In both the worlds of religion and science a certain kind of reductionistic Western mind is being forced to reframe itself.

The irony is that, today, religious people are often much more invested in either-or thinking than most scientists, who now know better. Many in academia have the humility to work with various theories and hypotheses, and move ahead "as if" an idea were true, until more of the mystery can be understood. Many of us, including clergy, want to have our certain conclusions without any prayer, honest study, suffering, waiting, or inner journey. We just want to "think" our way to God and be certain every step of the way, while still calling it faith.

As Sir Arthur Eddington said in a now-famous quote, "The universe is not only stranger than we imagined, but stranger than we *can* imagine!" David Finkelstein adds, "We haven't the capacity to imagine anything crazy enough to stand a chance of being right." Huston Smith, who has given us so much as a scholar of religion, notes that science "can glimpse a land across a river, but its methods do not enable it to enter that land."[60] Many scientists have the humility to know the same and are willing to wait, hold out, and hold on, which is to trust their early glimpse and wait for more clues. That is real faith. We nonscientists also have methods that can enable us to enter that land.

Ken Wilber is really the best teacher today in helping many of us to see much of this and to give us an "integral spirituality," as he calls it. Pick any book of his that fascinates you, and you will know why I as a Christian recommend him, although he would largely self-identify as a Buddhist. He is our postmodern Thomas Aquinas, and one of the best friends — and loving critics — that religion has ever had.[61]

WHAT IT MEANS TO FOLLOW JESUS

Although I am a Catholic Christian, I am impressed that all three of the great Asian religions — Hindu Vedanta, Mahayana Buddhism, and Chinese Taoism — build upon a worldview of nonduality and paradox.[62] Nor did Christianity overlook this identical insight. We merely said it in a different way — for example, as "the unitive way" or divine intimacy — because we believe in a relational and personal God. The Jewish people were invited to place this idea on their doorposts and on their foreheads: "The Lord our God is ONE" (Deuteronomy 6:4).

Nonduality is expressed differently in different schools, and I do not fully agree with them all, but in Christianity nonduality was not a philosophical principle, not pantheism in any form, nor a denial of necessary differences. The nondual paradox and mystery was for Christians a living person, an icon we could gaze upon and fall in love with. Jesus became "the pioneer and perfecter of our faith" (Hebrews 12:2), "the Mediator," "very God and very human" at the same time, who consistently said "follow me." He is the living paradox, calling us to imitate him, as we realize that "[he] and the Father are one" (John 10:30). In him, the great gaps are all overcome; all cosmic opposites are reconciled in him, as the author of Colossians (1:15–20) says.

The nondual principle is believed and taught by Christians as the mystery of the incarnation, which invites us to put together all the same contraries we see in Jesus. That makes me joyful to be a Christian. Already in the second century, St. Irenaeus, who might be considered the first Christian theologian, called it "the scandal of the incarnation." It has remained a scandal to this day.

Throughout most of our history, we could not or would not hold the opposites together. In most cases, people simply lacked the inner spiritual experience or the intellectual tools. We were largely unable to find the pattern that connected all the mysteries, even though it had been fully given to us in Jesus. We worshiped Jesus instead of following him. We made Jesus into a mere religion instead of a journey toward union with God. This shift made us into a religion of belonging instead of a religion of transformation. But despite our best attempts to run away, we are still and forever drawn into the mystery graciously, and in ways we cannot control — you as well as I.

One of the most subtle ways to avoid imitating someone is to put them on a pedestal, above and apart from us. When you accept that Jesus was not merely divine but human as well, you can begin to see how you are not separate from Jesus. Open yourself to recognizing the great paradoxes within Jesus. Then you can begin to hold those same opposites together within yourself.

CHAPTER TWENTY-ONE

What Every Good Leader Knows

The children of this world are more astute in dealing with their own kind than are the children of light. — LUKE 16:8

At times, spiritual wisdom does not harmonize well with the goals and practices of the world. But sometimes spiritual seekers take this truth too far, thinking that to be "spiritual" we have to be naive and simplistic and can't lead as well as others. At the same time, religious leaders often try to bypass the needed competencies because they believe their special status makes the training — whether skill sets or the work of spiritual growth — unnecessary.

In fact, there is no greater training for true leadership than living in the naked now. There, we can set aside our own mental constructs and lead situations even more imaginatively — with the clearer vision of one who lives beyond himself or herself. This is surely why some of Christianity's great mystics, such as Teresa of Avila, Catherine of Siena, and Ignatius of Loyola, were also first-rate leaders, motivators of others, and reformers of institutions.

Here are some insights into what every good, nondual leader knows and practices, whether in the workplace, at home, or in the classroom.

+ Good leaders are seers of alternatives.

◈ Good leaders move forward by influencing events and inspiring people more than by ordering or demanding.

doing — giving hope

* Good leaders know that every one-sided solution is doomed ahead of time to failure. It is never a final solution but only a postponement of the problem.

* Good leaders learn to study, discern, and search together with their people for solutions.

* Good leaders know that total dilemmas are very few. We create many dilemmas because we are internally stuck, attached, fearful, overidentified with our position, needy of winning the case, or unable to entertain even the partial truth that the other opinion might be offering.

* Good leaders search for a middle ground where the most people can find meaning; they work for win/win situations. (This is hard to do if you assume you are the higher, the more responsible, the in-charge, the senior, the more competent — or once you have made a harsh judgment about the other.)

* Good leaders know that there is no perfect solution. That is the lie and false promise of the dualistic mind, polarity, and all-or-nothing thinking.

* Good leaders know that seeking exclusive or overly rapid recourse to the law is an easy way out, and often just a sign of laziness or fear of taking responsibility.

* Good leaders know that the rule of law and obedience can inform you only about what is illegal or immoral; it cannot of itself lead you to God, truth, goodness, or beauty (Romans 3:20 and 7:7).

* Good leaders know that rapid recourse to the law might be seeking the will of God, but it might also be seeking to avoid

the responsibility, the necessary self-doubt, the darkness, and the prayer required to live in faith, hope, and love.

⊙ Good leaders know that when done well, compromise and consensus-seeking is not a way of abdicating essential values, but very often a way of seeking — and finding — other values, especially community-building, along with giving more people a personal investment in the outcome.

◆ Good leaders know that wisdom is "the art of the possible." The key question is no longer "How can I problem-solve now, and get this off my plate?" It is "How can this situation achieve good for the largest number and for the next generations?"

◆ Good leaders keep prayerfully offering new data, until they can work toward some consensus from all sides.

◆ Good leaders want to increase both freedom and owner-ship among the group — not just subservience, which will ultimately sabotage the work anyway.

⊙ Good leaders let people know the why of a decision, and show how that is consistent with the group's values.

In short, good leaders must have a certain capacity for non-polarity thinking and full-access knowing (*prayer*), a tolerance for ambiguity (*faith*), an ability to hold creative tensions (*hope*), and an ability to care (*love*) beyond their own personal advantage.

In your own life of leadership, whether in private or in public, meditate on this list from time to time. Ask yourself honestly which aspects of nondual leadership are your strongest, and make note, over time, of which ones become more natural for you as you grow in the contemplative gaze.

CHAPTER TWENTY-TWO

The Principle of Likeness
In the End, It All Comes Down to This

Deep calls unto Deep.
— PSALM 42:7

Be the change you want to see in the world.
— MOHANDAS GANDHI

To have a spiritual life is to recognize early on that there is always a similarity and coherence between the seer and the seen, the seekers and what they are capable of finding. You will seek only what you have partially already discovered and seen within yourself as desirable. Spiritual cognition is invariably re-cognition.

Call it the "Principle of Likeness," if you will. The enormous breakthrough is that when you honor and accept the divine image within yourself, you cannot help but see it in everybody else, too, and you know it is just as undeserved and unmerited as it is in you. That is why you stop judging, and that is how you start loving unconditionally and without asking whether someone is worthy or not. The breakthrough occurs at once, although the realization deepens and takes on greater conviction over time.

As we learned when looking at conversion, nondual people will see things in their wholeness and call forth the same unity in others, simply by being who they are. Wholeness (head, heart, and body, all present and positive) can see and call forth wholeness in others. This is why it is so pleasant to be around whole and holy people.

Dualistic or divided people, however, live in a split and fragmented world. They cannot accept or forgive certain parts of themselves. They cannot accept that God objectively dwells within them, as 1 Corinthians 3:16–17 states. This lack of forgiveness takes the forms of a tortured mind, a closed heart, or an inability to live calmly and proudly inside your own body. The fragmented mind sees parts, not wholes, in itself and others, and invariably it creates antagonism, reaction, fear, and resistance — "push-back" — from other people.

What you see is what you get. What you seek is also what you get.

We mend and renew the world by strengthening inside ourselves what we seek outside ourselves, and not by demanding it of others or trying to force it on others.

This truth may sound like the Law of Attraction that is so widely discussed today, and often called the "Secret," but there is one major difference. Perhaps, like many people, you use the Law of Attraction to draw to yourself the good things you want in life — love, a successful relationship, stability. This is fine as far as it goes. The true contemplative mind, however, does not deny the utter "facticity" of the outer world. In fact, much of its suffering comes from seeing and accepting things exactly as they are. The Secret seems to be saying that your mind creates the outer world. I am saying that *you do create your response to it, and that response, for all practical purposes, is your reality.*

- If you want others to be more loving, choose to love first.

- If you want a reconciled outer world, reconcile your own inner world.

- If you are working for peace out there, create it inside as well.

- If you notice other people's irritability, let go of your own.

- If you wish to find some outer stillness, find it within yourself.

- If you are working for justice, treat yourself justly, too.

- If you find yourself resenting the faults of others, stop resenting your own.

- If the world seems desperate, let go of your own despair.

- If you want a just world, start being just in small ways yourself.

- If your situation feels hopeless, honor the one spot of hope inside you.

- If you want to find God, then honor God within you, and you will always see God beyond you. For it is only God in you who knows where and how to look for God.

Some Eastern religions have called this *karma,* the correspondence between who you are and what you can make happen. But this truth is not found only in the East. Jesus said the same, almost exactly:

Do not judge and you will not be judged,
Do not condemn and you will not be condemned,
Grant pardon, and you will be pardoned,

Give, and there will be gifts for you. . . .
The amount you measure out is the amount you will be
given back. — Luke 6:36–38

Now you can finally understand the words of Matthew 7:8: "Seek and you will find, knock and the door will be opened for you." Your desire to seek — even your interest in reading books such as this one — reflects a part of who you already are. *You desire only what you have already partially found.* The fact that you have read this book, and persevered to the end, means the Great Work has already begun in you!

APPENDICES

Practicing the Naked Now

APPENDIX 1 / LEVELS OF DEVELOPMENT

One of the more important breakthroughs in understanding why some people seem to "get it" (whatever "it" is) while many do not get it or even oppose or distort it, has now come to be recognized by teachers as diverse as Jean Piaget, Lawrence Kohlberg, Abraham Maslow, James Fowler, Clare Grave, and Ken Wilber. Their insights remind us of Thomas Aquinas's observation that "Whatever is received, is received according to the mode of the receiver."

In simple terms, whatever you teach or receive will be heard on at least eight to ten different levels, according to the inner, psychological, and spiritual maturity of the listener. Level 1 people will misuse the Bible, the sacraments, the priesthood, spiritual direction, the Enneagram, or anything else that is presented to them. Levels 7–9 people will make lemonade out of even sour or unripe lemons (although not without price).

It does little good merely to assert doctrines or passages of Scripture and, because people assent to them, to assume that they have any existential knowledge of what they are talking about. You can perfectly assent to the Catholic belief in the Real Presence, for example, and be totally incapable of presence yourself — so there will be no inner experience and no transformation of the self. One will manipulate or use the very doctrine for ego enhancement purposes and control. This is likely what Jesus is referring to when he quotes Isaiah 29:13 in his Sermon on the Mount: "This people has all the right words, but no change of heart. It is all just a lesson memorized, a human commandment."

My own attempt to correlate the various schemas of development that I have studied would have me put it this way. In my experience, we move from level 1 to level 9. (Note that this is merely a teaching tool; real life is much more subtle.)

1. **My body and self-image are who I am.** Leads to a dominance of security, safety, and defense needs. Dualistic/polarity thinking.

2. **My external behavior is who I am.** Needs to look good outside and to hide or disguise the contrary evidence from others; I become so practiced at this game that the evidence is eventually hidden from myself, too. This *emergence of the shadow* is very common among conservatives.

3. **My thoughts/feelings are who I am.** Development of intellect and will to have better thoughts and feelings and also control them so others do not know, and so, finally, that I do not see their self-serving and shadowy character myself. This *education as a substitute for transformation* is very common among liberals and the educated.

Normally a major defeat, shock, or humiliation must be suffered and passed through to go beyond this stage.

4. **My deeper intuitions and felt knowledge in my body are who I am.** This is such a breakthrough and so informative and helpful that many become stymied at this level. Leads to individualism, self-absorption, and inner work as a substitute for any real encounter with otherness.

5. **My shadow self is who I am.** *The dark night.* My weakness comes to overwhelm me, as I face myself in my raw, unvarnished, uncivilized state. Without guidance, grace, and prayer, most go running back to previous identities. Time is of the essence here.

6. **I am empty and powerless.** "God's Waiting Room." Almost any attempt to save the self by any superior behavior, technique, morality, positive role, or religious devotion will lead to regression. All you can do is wait and ask and trust. Here is where you learn faith and discover that darkness is the much better teacher. God is about to become real.

7. **I am much more than who I thought I was.** Death of the false self, and birth of the True Self. But because you are not at home here yet, it will first of all feel like a *void*, even if a wonderful void. "Luminous darkness," as John of the Cross would call it.

8. **"I and the Father are one"** (John 10:30). Henceforth there is only God, or as Teresa says, *"One knows God in oneself, and knows oneself in God."* All else is seen as a passing ego possession, and I do not need to protect it, promote it, or prove it — to anyone.

9. **I am who I am** — "just me." Warts and all, enough to be human, no window dressing necessary. This is the most radical critique of religion possible, because now you know religion is just a finger pointing to the moon, but not the moon itself. There is no need to *appear* to be anything but who I really am. Fully detached from self-image and living in God's image of you — which includes and loves both the good and the bad. The serenity and freedom of the saints. Total Nonduality.

The goal is to keep people moving deeper into faith, knowing they will receive any and all information and experience at their level.

APPENDIX 2 / TRAINING FOR THE "THIRD EYE"

The lamp of the body is the eye.
— Matthew 6:22

The ego self is the unobserved self. If you do not find an objective standing point from which to look back at yourself, you will almost always be egocentric — identified with yourself instead of in relationship to yourself.

Most of us have been given no training or practice in this, because we thought it was all negative self-criticism instead of calm self-observation (moral examination of *conscience* instead of examination of *consciousness*). Ego is not bad; it is just what takes over when you do not see truthfully and completely. That "lamp" does not illuminate things well.

Much of the early work of contemplation is finding that stance and learning how to return there in all moments of emotional turmoil (positive as much as negative), until you can eventually live more and more of your life there. You will find yourself smiling, sighing, and "weeping" at yourself, more than either hating or congratulating yourself (which of themselves are both ego needs).

Eventually, you will discover a detached place of quiet self-observation.

* It must be without moral judgment, or you will tire of it and rebel against it.

* It must be compassionate and calmly objective.

* It names the moment for what it is.

* It names my reaction without a need to praise or blame — it just sees it.

* To see my reaction for what it is, it takes away this reaction's addictive and self-serving character.

* It deflates my reaction and disempowers it from "possessing" me.

* Now I have a feeling instead of a feeling having me.

* It maintains the good sense of "I" but without ego attachment.

* It actually fosters much deeper, broader, more honest feelings.

* It also gives me a strong sense of "I," because there is now no need to totally eliminate or deny the negative part. (My full self is accepted.)

* Ironically, the truly destructive part of the negative is exposed and falls away as now unnecessary. To see the negative is to defeat it, for evil relies upon denial and disguise.

The Christian name for this stable witness is the Holy Spirit:

- already in place, and doing all the giving; filling in all the gaps
- already compassionate and more merciful than we are
- never demanding the perfection of any technique, practice, or asceticism.

One only needs to constantly connect with our deepest level of desiring, which, paradoxically, is much harder than mere will power and technique. *The Spirit bears common witness with our spirit that we are indeed children of God* (Romans 8:16). It is a common knowing, a participative event, and feels like you are being "known through," but with total acceptance and forgiveness. This will change your life! You will then "know as fully as you are known" (1 Corinthians 13:12).

APPENDIX 3 / LITANY OF THE HOLY SPIRIT

When I did a hermitage in the Lent of 2006 in Arizona, I had an enduring sense of the presence and the guidance of the Holy Spirit, one that I think is fully available to all of us "if we but knew the gift of God" (John 4:10). I slowly composed this prayer litany to awaken and strengthen this Presence within you. Recite it whenever you are losing faith in God or in yourself.

Pure Gift of God
Indwelling Presence
Promise of the Father
Life of Jesus
Pledge and Guarantee
Eternal Praise
Defense Attorney
Inner Anointing
Reminder of the Mystery
Homing Device
Knower of All Things
Stable Witness
Implanted Pacemaker
Overcomer of the Gap
Always Already Awareness
Compassionate Observer
Magnetic Center
God Compass
Inner Breath
Divine DNA
Mutual Yearning Place
Given Glory
Hidden Love of God
Choiceless Awareness
Implanted Hope
Seething Desire
Fire of Life and Love
Sacred Peacemaker
Nonviolence of God
Seal of the Incarnation
First Fruits of Everything
Father and Mother of Orphans

Planted Law
Truth Speaker
God's Secret Plan
Great Bridge Builder
Warmer of Hearts
Space between Everything
Flowing Stream
Wind of Change
Descending Dove
Cloud of Unknowing
Uncreated Grace
Filled Emptiness
Through-Seer
Deepest Level of Our Longing
Attentive Heart
Sacred Wounding
Holy Healing
Softener of Our Spirit
Will of God
Great Compassion
Generosity of the Creator
Inherent Victory
The One Sadness
Our Shared Joy
God's Tears
God's Happiness
The Welcoming Within
New and Eternal Covenant
Contract Written on Our Hearts
Jealous Lover
Desiring of God

*You who pray in us, through us, with us,
for us, and in spite of us. Amen. Alleluia!*

1. With your *senses* (not so much your mind), focus on one single object until you stop fighting it or resisting it with other concerns.

   The concrete is the doorway to the universal. This is the basic principle of the Incarnation, and Duns Scotus's theory of "thisness" — or even Tolle's teaching of the "power of now."

   This should lead to *an initial calmness in your body and mind.*

2. You must *choose not* to judge the object in any way, attach to it, reject it as meaningless, like it or dislike it. This is merely the need of the ego to categorize and control and define itself by preferences.

   You will thus learn to appreciate and respect things in and for themselves, and not because they either profit you or threaten you.

   This should lead to *a kind of subtle, simple JOY in the object itself* and also within yourself.

3. "Listen" to the object and allow it to speak to you. Allow a simple dialogue to happen. Speak back to it with respect and curiosity.

   You will thus learn to stop "objectifying" things as merely for your own consumption, control, or use. You are learning to allow things to take the initiative and speak their truth to you as a receiver instead of the giver.

   This will lead to *the beginnings of LOVE for the object or event, and a sense of loving kindness within yourself.*

4. A kind of *contented spaciousness* and *silence* will normally ensue. This is a form of nondual consciousness.

   The concrete, loving consciousness of one thing leads to pure consciousness or "objectless consciousness" of all things (the contemplative mind as such).

   Only after the fact does one look back and realize it was a holy/whole moment. If you do it during the moment itself, it spoils the pure experience, because ego with its judgments and attachments has reentered the scene.

APPENDIX 5 / CHRISTIAN TANTRA: THE "WELLING UP" EXERCISE

This exercise is based on a teaching from Fray Francisco de Osuna, O.F.M. (1492–1542), the spiritual "master" of Teresa of Avila. Here is what he taught his students:

1. Dam up the fountain of your soul, where love is always springing forth.

2. It will be forced to rise.

3. Yet it will remain quiet and at rest within you; wait for that quiet.

4. You will see the image of God reflected in your own clear waters, more resplendent than in any other thing — provided the disturbing turmoil of thoughts dies down.

   The following is only a commentary and aid on that teaching, so that you can experience it for yourself. It is really quite similar to what the Hindus discovered in tantra, where you hold the powerful gift and do not express it, so that it can be deepened and refined. I think it is also what Jesus is offering the Samaritan woman when he says to her: "The water that I shall give you will turn into a spring inside of you, welling up into limitless life." (John 4:14)

1. Try to stay *beneath* your thoughts, neither fighting them nor thinking them.

2. Hold yourself at a deeper level, perhaps in your chest, solar plexus, or breath, but stay in your *body self* somehow, and do not rise to the mind. *Everything you know long-term, you know in your body.*

3. Resist any desire to repress or express, just animal contentment.

4. It will feel exactly like "nothing" or just darkness.

5. Stay "crouched" there at the cellular level without shame.

6. Long enough for Another Source to begin to flow.

7. And *well up* as light or sight or joy. This is the "super-essential life."

8. From this place you *become seeing,* and the love flows through you from the Source, as an energy more than an idea.

9. You cannot "think" God. God is never an "object" of consciousness like any other thing, person, or event that you "know." God is always and forever the subject, the doer, the initiator, "the Prevenient Grace."

10. *You have then "become" what you hope to see.* Subject and object are one. God in you and through you, sees and loves God.

APPENDIX 6 / THE PRAYER OF THE SELF-EMPTYING ONE

Philippians 2:6–11 is thought to be an early Christian hymn to the Christ journey: a path of *kenosis* (self-emptying), incarnating in the "slave," "as all humans are," and even all the way to the bottom of total "acceptance" and "even humbler yet" (the cross). This allows God to raise Jesus up in God's time and God's way, and "name" him anew in a glorious state of transformation.

This hymn can be taken as a rather precise guide for the process of contemplative prayer, if we apply to the soul the same mystery that was in Christ Jesus. As mentioned throughout the book, take it as a rule: *"Everything we can say of Jesus, we can say also about the soul."* This is exactly how he becomes the icon of transformation for us, and why he says "follow me."

Notice how it begins with this verse:

"In your minds you must be the same as Christ Jesus...."

1. Your "state" is also divine. Hold it confidently (the True Self in God).

2. But do not cling to it with any form of self-validation or importance.

3. Instead, "empty yourself" and refuse to self-name — either up or down, positively or negatively.

4. Enter fully into your humble human state of failure and weakness, even to the point of complete detachment, if called to or if possible.

5. Now God can pick you up at the right time, when God is ready.

6. God can "name" you correctly, secretly, truthfully, and always lovingly, *by* Him and *as* His (Experienced True Self).

7. This Self is indestructible, un-offendable, and already in heaven.

Note that shortly thereafter, there is a final affirming and confirming passage:

> It is God who for God's own loving purpose *puts both this will and this action into you.* (2:13)

Even the sitting down, dying for twenty minutes, and still standing up afterward is a perfect metaphor for what is happening in prayer — always the mystery of death and resurrection.

APPENDIX 7 / THE VIRGIN PRAYER

God regarded her in her lowliness.
— Luke 1:48

You must seek to be a blank slate.
You must desire to remain unwritten on.
No choosing of this or that.
Not "I am good because."

Nor "I am not good because."
Neither excitement nor boredom.

Remaining Nothing,
An unchosen virgin,
And unchoosing too, just empty.
No story line by which to start the day.
No identity enhancers nor losses
To make yourself valuable or not.

Nothing interesting, nothing uninteresting.
Neither against, nor for something.
Nothing to recall from yesterday.
Nothing to look forward to today.

Just me, naked, exposed,
No self to fix, change or find,
Nothing to judge right or wrong,
Important or unimportant,
Worthy or unworthy,
I stand and wait,
neither powerful nor powerless,

For You to name me,
For You to look upon my face,
For You to write my script,
For You to give the kiss,
In your time and your way.

You always do.
And it is always so much better.

"And she gave birth to her firstborn" (Luke 2:7), who was the
Christ.

APPENDIX 8 / WALKING MEDITATION: THE MIRROR MEDALLION

Toward the end of my Lenten hermitage in 2003, I began to have a very dynamic experience of the Trinity, as a movement through me, in me, and out of me. I so wanted to thank God for all I had been given during those days, and I realized that the only way I could fittingly thank God was to offer God back to God, just as is happening in the Trinity. I wanted to become the very willing relay station for the breath of God.

Each evening I took a long walk down a steep hill and back up again. Of course, I began to breathe heavily on the return, and I gradually conformed my breath to my steps. I found myself saying the word "beauty" as I took *in* each breath, and then "back" as I breathed *out.* Again and again, "Beauty...Back... Beauty...Back." It soon became my form of walking meditation.

I knew the phrase had come from a line from my favorite poet, the Jesuit Gerard Manley Hopkins. In his lesser-known poem "The Golden Echo" he said:

> ... Deliver it early now, long before death.
> Give beauty back, beauty, beauty, beauty back to
> God, beauty's self and beauty's giver.

In "Morning, Midday, and Evening Sacrifice," he says,

> This, all this beauty blooming,
> This, all this freshness fuming,
> Give God while worth consuming.

I began to think of some way that I could help others to participate in this wonderful flow of life through me. It seemed like a living experience of the Trinity: we are the embodied Christ and the Tabernacle of the Holy Spirit, giving praise to the Father by our very existence. I pictured wearing a "mirror medallion" that would take in all scenes in front of me moment by moment. It would not look like a piece of religious jewelry, but merely a plain mirror that always takes in exactly what it sees, without distortion or judgment or analysis, only love.

The back of the mirror would have an image of the EYE OF GOD forever gazing at me with love, respect, and even desire. I had recently come across a largely ignored passage in James 4:5: It said, "The longing of the Spirit that He sent to dwell in us is a jealous longing." Let's be a part of that deep and conscious longing for God!

In India, they have the notion of *darshan*: the Hindus go to the temple, not to see God, statues, or rituals, as much as to be seen by God! This mirror medallion could help us to allow God to look at us as we are, to gaze at us, to delight in us!

So this medallion is to educate you in the flow, in the ability *to both receive and reflect back the glory of God,* which is why I chose the quote from 2 Corinthians 3:18 for the back. It is actually an exercise in passivity, in allowing, in surrendering, in enjoying what is already happening. Now the eye of God, gazing inwardly at your breast, will be a constant reminder of what is already happening. It will hold you in the Eternal Now and in the flow that is the very life of the Trinity.[63]

Joy and mind. Those are not words that you would normally put together, but they inspired the eleventh-century Richard of St. Victor, a Scottish canon teaching in Paris, and became the themes of his two books on the contemplative mind, *Benjamin Major* and *Benjamin Minor*. The titles are taken from one obscure passage from Psalm 68:27, where "Benjamin" is described as leading a procession into the temple *in mentis excessu*, which was translated as "with a joyful mind" or "with an ecstatic mind." This made me ask:

What might a joyful mind be?

When your mind does not need to be right.

When you no longer need to compare yourself with others.

When you no longer need to compete — not even in your own head.

When your mind can be creative, but without needing anyone to know.

When you can live in contentment with whatever the moment offers.

When you do not need to analyze or judge things in or out, positive or negative.

When your mind does not need to be in charge, but can serve the moment with gracious and affirming information.

When your mind follows the intelligent lead of your heart.

When your mind is curious and interested, not suspicious and interrogating.

When your mind does not "brood over injuries."

When you do not need to humiliate, critique, or defeat those who have hurt you — not even in your mind.

When your mind does not need to create self-justifying story lines.

When your mind does not need the future to be better than today.

When your mind can let go of obsessive or negative thoughts.

When your mind can think well of itself, but without needing to.

When your mind can accept yourself as you are, warts and all.

When your mind can surrender to what is.

When your mind does not divide and always condemn one side or group.

When your mind can find truth on both sides.

When your mind fills in the gaps with "the benefit of the doubt" for both friend and enemy.

When your mind can critique and also detach from the critique.

When your mind can wait, listen, and learn.

When your mind can live satisfied without resolution or closure.

When your mind can forgive and actually "forget."

When your mind can admit it was wrong and change.

When your mind can stop judging and critiquing itself.

When you don't need to complain or worry to get motivated.

When you can observe your mind contracting into self-preservation or self-validation, and then laugh or weep over it.

When you can actually love with your mind.

When your mind can find God in all things.

THE SHINING WORD "AND"

"And" teaches us to say yes

"And" allows us to be *both–and*

"And" keeps us from *either–or*

"And" teaches us to be patient and long-suffering

"And" is willing to wait for insight and integration

"And" keeps us from dualistic thinking

"And" does not divide the field of the moment

"And" helps us to live in the always imperfect now

"And" keeps us inclusive and compassionate toward everything

"And" demands that our contemplation become action

"And" insists that our action is also contemplative

"And" heals our racism, sexism, heterosexism, and classism

"And" keeps us from the false choice of liberal *or* conservative

"And" allows us to critique both sides of things

"And" allows us to enjoy both sides of things

"And" is far beyond any one nation or political party

"And" helps us face and accept our own dark side

"And" allows us to ask for forgiveness and to apologize

"And" is the mystery of paradox in all things

"And" is the way of mercy

"And" makes daily, practical love possible

"And" does not trust love if it is not also justice

"And" does not trust justice if it is not also love

"And" is far beyond my religion versus your religion

"And" allows us to be both distinct and yet united

"And" is the very Mystery of Trinity

Notes

1. Gregory Wolfe, *The New Religious Humanists* (New York: Free Press, 1997), 128.

2. James Alison, *Undergoing God: Dispatches from the Scene of a Break-In* (New York: Continuum, 2006).

3. John J. Prendergast, ed., *The Sacred Mirror: Nondual Wisdom and Psychotherapy* (St. Paul, Minn.: Paragon, 2003). Also, absolutely *anything* by Gerald May is superb and timeless. Gerald was a dear personal friend and a true holy man.

4. I have included a Litany to the Holy Spirit on page 168 of this book. This can be a practice to help you draw upon this infallible Source within you.

5. See Richard Rohr, "The Divine Dance," recorded conference on the centrality and implications of God as a Trinity of persons, available at *cacradicalgrace.org*.

6. David Abram, *The Spell of the Sensuous* (New York: Random House, 1996), 249–50.

7. See Appendix 1.

8. *Richard of St. Victor*, Classics of Western Spirituality (New York: Paulist Press, 1979), De Sacramentis, I,X,ii, and The Mystical Ark (Benjamin Major), III–IV.

9. See David Berreby, *Us and Them: The Science of Identity* (Chicago: University of Chicago Press, 2005).

10. Aldous Huxley, *The Perennial Philosophy* (New York: Harper, 1945), 294–95.

11. Jim Marion, *Putting on the Mind of Christ* (Charlottesville, Va.: Hampton Roads Publishing, 2000), 197ff. Cynthia Bourgeault, *Centering Prayer and Inner Awakening* (Cambridge, Mass.: Cowley, 2004), 69ff. Also Cynthia Bourgeault, *The Wisdom Way of Knowing* (San Francisco: Jossey-Bass, 2003).

12. Ken Wilber, *One Taste: The Journals of Ken Wilber* (Boston: Shambala, 2000), 25ff.

13. Amy-Jill Levine, *The Misunderstood Jew: The Church and the Scandal of the Jewish Jesus* (San Francisco: Harper One, 2006), 17ff.; John Meier, *A Marginal Jew: Rethinking the Historical Jesus* (New York: Doubleday, 2001).

14. Kathleen Warren, *Daring to Cross the Threshold* (Rochester, Minn.: Sisters of St. Francis, 2003).

15. Owen Barfield, *Saving the Appearances: A Study in Idolatry* (New York: Harcourt Brace, 1957), 40ff.

16. See schema in Appendix 1.

17. Bonaventure, *Opera Omnia*, V, 38b.

18. See, among others, the schemas of Spiral Dynamics from the research of Clare Graves; the Integral Spirituality of Ken Wilber; or the "mansions" of St. Teresa of Avila — not to mention almost all religions of the East and near East, which Jesus also represented.

19. Gerald May, *Will and Spirit* (San Francisco: HarperSanFrancisco, 1982), 1.

20. Walter Wink, *The Human Being: Jesus and the Enigma of the Son of the Man* (Minneapolis: Fortress, 2002), 22–23.

21. Thorleif Boman, *Hebrew Thought Compared to Greek* (New York: Norton, 1960). This is a quite scholarly book that can leave you somewhat humbled with regard to our scriptural certitudes about what Jesus always meant.

22. Thomas Keating, Richard Rohr, fully recorded conference "The Eternal Now," 1996, *cacradicalgrace.org*.

23. Philip Gulley and James Mulholland, *If God Is Love* (San Francisco: Harper One, 2004). A brilliant, honest book that was a long time in coming.

24. Berreby, *Us and Them.*

25. Richard Rohr, O.F.M., *Things Hidden: Scripture as Spirituality* (Cincinnati: St. Anthony Messenger, 2007), chapter 1.

26. See Appendix 1.

27. Bernard Lonergan: *A Second Collection* (Philadelphia: Westminster Press, 1975), 71.

28. Chet Raymo, *When God Is Gone Everything Is Holy: The Making of a Religious Naturalist* (Notre Dame, Ind.: Sorin Books, 2008), 25ff.

29. Lonergan, *A Second Collection*, 79.

30. Bernard Lonergan, *Method in Theology* (New York: Seabury Press, 1979), 270.

31. Ibid., 242.

32. Lonergan, *A Second Collection,* 67.

33. See exercise in Appendix 2 to practice this seeing.

34. Paula D'Arcy and Richard Rohr, "Spirituality for the Two Halves of Life," recorded conference, 2003, *cacradicalgrace.org.*

35. As discussed elsewhere, it took us, for example, till the last century to *begin* to face our anti-Semitism, our rather universal racism, our classism, and our normal alignment with power, war, and money. Only now are we beginning to recognize our sexism and homophobia. "Guts, guns, and glory" were fully in charge in "Christian" nations during their conquest of the new world. Now the recent "crisis of prosperity" is forcing us to recognize the depth of our complicity with Western greed and consumerism. Jesus was too much for us. I wonder how many of us could even now think of the failures of our banks and financial system as a work of the Holy Spirit?

36. This is what Brian McLaren calls "religion as an evacuation plan for the next world."

37. General audience, July 28, 1999.

38. Marion, *Putting on the Mind of Christ,* 13ff.

39. Richard Rohr, *Everything Belongs* (New York: Crossroad, 1999), passim.

40. Richard Rohr, *Adam's Return* (New York: Crossroad, 2004), 60ff.

41. Mary Beth Ingham and Richard Rohr, "Holding the Tension: The Power of Paradox," 2007, recorded conference, *cacradicalgrace.org.*

42. Bruno Barnhart, *The Future of Wisdom* (New York: Continuum, 2007), 13ff., and *Second Simplicity* (Mahwah, N.J.: Paulist, 1999), 61ff. Both books are brilliant analyses of what we have in the tradition, what we have lost, and how we can regain it.

43. Hugo Lassalle, *Living in the New Consciousness* (Boston: Shambala, 1988), 139.

44. Thomas Merton, *The Hidden Ground of Love: The Letters of Thomas Merton on Religious Experience and Social Concern,* ed. William Henry Shannon (New York: Farrar, Straus, Giroux, 1985), 341.

45. I invite you to examine the works of John Main, Bede Griffiths, Thomas Keating, Cynthia Bourgeault, Bruno Barnhart, Laurence Freeman, Ruth Barrows, Bernadette Roberts, Eckhart Tolle, Jean-Yves Leloup, Sebastian Painadath, Hugo Enomiya-Lassalle, and Ken Wilber who each in their own way are recovering the older tradition today.

46. Teresa of Avila, *Vida,* chapter 4.

47. Francisco de Osuna, *The Third Spiritual Alphabet* (New York: Paulist, 1981), or a fine summary in Harvey Egan, *An Anthology of Christian Mysticism* (Collegeville, Minn.: Liturgical Press, 1991), 413–22. I am happy to reintroduce the overlooked de Osuna to my own Franciscan world, although I studied him in my own novitiate in 1961.

48. St. Bonaventure, *The Soul's Journey to God* (New York: Paulist, 1978). Chapter 7 of this classic that we studied seemed to me like impossible abstraction and poetry until I discovered for myself what Bonaventure called "the training of the mind to reach the Sabbath of rest" where "all intellectual activities must be left behind" (110ff.).

49. It is often an "anti-sign" to be celibate if you are still very dualistic in your thought patterns. People see us as mean, judgmental, or narcissistic instead of transformed. True contemplatives are very different kinds of human beings, and I suppose monks and nuns, ascetics and sadhus were supposed to be the wisdom people who kept this supremely important consciousness alive in society, as in Buddhism, Hinduism, and medieval Christianity.

50. The World Community for Christian Meditation, based on the work of John Main and Laurence Freeman, and Contemplative Outreach, based on the work of Thomas Keating, are the best known and most systematic teaching of a Christian contemplative practice today.

51. Vatican II, *Dei Verbum* I, 2–6.

52. Jean Pierre De Caussade, *Abandonment to Divine Providence* (Garden City, N.Y.: Image Books, 1975); Brother Lawrence, *The Practice of the Presence of God: Conversations and Letters of Brother Lawrence* (Oxford: Oneworld, 1999). These two books are the classics here that taught us how to be present in the present and to the Presence. See also Thomas Keating and Richard Rohr, "The Eternal Now," recorded conference, 2004, *cacradicalgrace.org.*

53. Marianne Williamson, *Healing the Soul of America* (New York: Simon & Schuster, 1997); Katie Byron, *A Thousand Names for Joy* (New York: Harmony, 2007). These two spiritually brilliant women are perhaps the finest contemporary examples of nondual thinking that affects their entire worldview. They will change your lives and could change society, if heard.

54. Barnhart, *The Future of Wisdom,* 31ff.

55. Richard Rohr, "The Cosmic Christ," 2008, recorded conference, available at *cacradicalgrace.org.*

56. Barnhart, *The Future of Wisdom,* 91 and throughout.

57. Russ Hudson and Richard Rohr, O.F.M., "Laughing and Weeping: The Enneagram as a Tool for Non-Dual Consciousness," recorded conference, *cacradicalgrace.org.*

58. "The Divine Dance" and "The Shape of God," recorded conferences on the momentous implications of the doctrine of Trinity, *cacradicalgrace.org.*

59. Here are some of the key authors in this direction: Rev. John Polkinghorne, Aileen O'Donoghue, Sr. Ilia Delio, Thomas Berry, Jim Shenk, Hans Küng, Judy Cannato, Miriam Therese Winter, Diarmuid O'Murchu, Bernard Haisch.

60. Huston Smith, *Forgotten Truth* (San Francisco: HarperSanFrancisco, 1992), 116.

61. In Ken Wilber, "One Two Three of God," for example, read his "Spirit in the 2nd Person," and you will think you are reading a classic Christian mystic. Ken Wilber, *Integral Spirituality: A Startling New Role for Religion in the Modern and Postmodern World* (Boston: Integral Books, 2007), 159–60.

62. David Loy, *Nonduality: A Study in Comparative Philosophy* (New Haven, Conn.: Yale University Press, 1988).

63. This simple medallion can be ordered at *cacradicalgrace.org,* at the Resource Center.

Center for
Action and Contemplation

Our Vision

The Center for Action and Contemplation supports
a new reformation from the inside!

* In the spirit of the Gospels
* Confirming people's deeper spiritual intuitions
* Encouraging actions of justice rooted in prayer
* With a new appreciation for, and cooperation with, other denominations, religions, and cultures

Our Mission

"We are a center for experiential education, encouraging the transformation of human consciousness through contemplation, equipping people to be instruments of peaceful change in the world."

For up-to-date information on the Center's
conferences, internships, and available resources,
visit *www.cacradicalgrace.org.*

Of Related Interest

Richard Rohr and Friends
CONTEMPLATION IN ACTION

Where else can you find spiritual inspiration from
Richard Rohr, Jim Wallis, Thomas Keating, Basil Pen-
nington, Paula D'Arcy, and others in one accessible
volume? This book, designed for bedside reading,
offers the best of Richard Rohr's *Radical Grace* news-
letter, along with new meditations from new and
established authors.

0-8245-2388-1, paperback

Richard Rohr
THE GOOD NEWS ACCORDING TO LUKE
Spiritual Reflections

Grounded in scholarship but accessible to a general
audience, this spiritual commentary sheds light on the
main themes of Luke's Gospel. Rohr addresses individual concerns, duties, and possibilities, and then
connects them to the larger picture of cultural and
ecclesial postures, emphases, and values.

0-8245-1966-3, paperback

Of Related Interest

Richard Rohr
EVERYTHING BELONGS
The Gift of Contemplative Prayer

Revised & Updated!

A personal retreat for those who hunger for a deeper prayer life but don't know what contemplation really is or how to let it happen.

Richard Rohr has written this book to help us pray better and see life differently. Using parables, koans, and personal experiences, he leads us beyond the techniques of prayer to a place where we can receive the gift of contemplation: the place where (if only for a moment) we see the world in God clearly, and know that everything belongs.

"Rohr at his finest: insightful cultural critique — with strong connection to the marginalized."
— *The Other Side*

0-8245-1995-7, paperback

Of Related Interest

Fr. Timothy Gallagher, O.M.V.
THE EXAMEN PRAYER
Ignatian Wisdom for Our Lives Today

With a foreword by Fr. George Aschenbrenner

This is the first book to explain the examen prayer, one of the most popular practices in Christian spirituality. Fr. Timothy Gallagher takes us deep into the prayer, showing that the prayer Ignatius of Loyola believed to be at the center of the spiritual life is just as relevant to our lives today.

Topics include: Desire ~ A Day with Ignatius ~ Gratitude ~ Petition ~ Review ~ Discernment ~ Forgiveness ~ Our Image of God ~ The Future ~ Flexibility ~ The Freedom of the Spirit ~ The Contemplative Capacity ~ Journaling ~ Renewal ~ Courage ~ Spiritual Consolation ~ Letting Go ~ Fruits ~ Discerning Awareness throughout the Day

0-8245-2367-9, paperback